Alison Wilson (née McKelvie) was born in 1920 and raised in Cumbria. She moved to London during the war, where she worked as a secretary in the Intelligence Service. In 1963, Alison converted to Catholicism and studied Catholic theology at Heythrop College, Oxford, gaining the STL (Licenciate in Sacred Theology) and Bachelor of Divinity, the first laywoman to have done so in England. She combined her devotional life with her role as mother, grand-mother and great-grandmother to an ever-growing family, and lived her latter years in Addlestone, Surrey, where she died aged eighty-four.

She wrote the story of her life in 1986, and disclosed the first half to her sons in 1992, having kept its secrets for thirty years. The second half was discovered only after Alison's death in 2005. Her story was the basis of the three-part BBC drama, *Mrs Wilson*, in which the role of Alison was played by her granddaughter, actress Ruth Wilson.

BEFORE & AFTER

*The Incredible Story
of the Real-life Mrs Wilson*

ALISON WILSON

CONSTABLE

CONSTABLE

First published in Great Britain in 2019 by Constable
This paperback edition published in 2020

13 5 7 9 10 8 6 4 2

A CIP catalogue record for this book is available from the British Library.

ISBN: 978-1-47213-235-2

Typeset in Palatino by Hewer Text UK Ltd, Edinburgh
Printed and bound in Great Britain by Clays Ltd, Elcograf S.p.A.

Papers used by Constable are from well-managed
forests and other responsible sources.

Constable
An imprint of
Little, Brown Book Group
Carmelite House
50 Victoria Embankment
London EC4Y 0DZ

An Hachette UK Company
www.hachette.co.uk

www.littlebrown.co.uk

Foreword by Gordon and Nigel Wilson

In March 1993 our mother, Alison Wilson, presented us with a document she wanted us to read. It turned out to be the 'Before' section of her extraordinary life story, the second part of which we would not see until after our mother's death in 2005. Having reflected long and hard on the right time to reveal the truth, she had invited us to dinner and given each of us a copy of the first part of the text she had written, six years earlier, while sequestered at a Carmelite Monastery in Wales. What we learned that night turned our view of our own lives – and that of our parents – upside down. We discovered that Alec – our father, and our mother's beloved husband – had not only been a prolific thriller writer and an MI6 agent but also, shockingly, a bigamist. The two 'distant cousins' who had attended our father's funeral were, in fact, our half-brothers. Completely stunned by the revelations, at this point we did not try and contact them. However, all that was to change later, as further unsettling information came to light.

Our mother, Alison McKelvie, was born on 6 August 1920 in Moresby, Cumberland (as Cumbria was then known). Most of her young life was spent in Drigg, near Whitehaven, where her father George McKelvie practised as a solicitor. She first met Alec – Alexander Wilson – in 1940, when she was working at what is now called MI6, intercepting all the telephone calls from foreign missions in London. Thrown together in the war-torn capital, Alison quickly fell in love with her dashing suitor. 'He was likeable, kind, gentle, quiet, abstemious . . .' Alec made no secret of the fact he had been married and had a son aged around ten, but claimed that his wife had walked out on him and that his divorce was being finalised. He had connections to the prestigious dukes of Marlborough, he told Alison's parents; he owned a large house but it had been requisitioned, he said, to explain why it would not be available until after the war.

In the heightened atmosphere of a London under attack by German bombers, the relationship between Alec and our mother developed rapidly. Having miraculously survived a direct hit on her flat Alison, now homeless, moved into Alec's boarding house. They soon became lovers. Alec, under pressure from Alison to extricate himself from his previous relationship, eventually claimed, falsely as it turned out, that the divorce had been granted. Our mother was pregnant with Gordon when, on 8th September 1941, she and Alec got married in a Catholic church.

The story of what happened next was set out in the remarkable document that our mother handed us that evening in 1992 and which is now reproduced here. For both of us the revelations were at once shocking and intensely moving. For the first time we were able to gain an understanding as to the extent of her sacrifices and suffering, and of her extraordinary sense of integrity, duty and responsibility. Amid all the other emotions that swirled through us that evening, we both felt incredibly blessed to have had a mother who, in a quiet, undemonstrative way, had shown such exceptional strength of character and purpose. Despite the hugely adverse circumstances in which she found herself, Alison had given us a rock-solid foundation from which to embark on our own lives, a security and stability that came at enormous physical, emotional and mental cost to her. We are both very conscious that we owe everything that we are today to her.

If we had been asked, when growing up, what our mother most loved, apart from her family, we would probably have said three things: poetry, Cumberland and horses. We remember how delighted she was whenever we saw a horse on our rural walks. She used occasionally to go out to ride, sometimes on Rotten Row in Hyde Park, usually with her best friend from school, Judith. Gordon remembers well her love of poetry in his younger years and after her death he recovered from her files several large exercise books full of poems, mostly by other authors, but also some she wrote herself. She always spoke so eloquently of her love of Cumberland, which imbued in us too a love of the region. In 1966 we went, together with Gordon's fiancée, for a delightful summer holiday, driving and walking around Cumberland. She regaled us with tales about her life as a young girl in the county, and we could all see the pleasure she took in revisiting it. Years before, as schoolboys, we had been invited to spend a month every summer in the magnificent house belonging to Gordon's godmother, who was like a real fairy godmother to us.

For our mother these must have been brief moments of light and luxury in a life with precious little of either. Alec was a maverick character; the persona he had adopted of a highly respected retired Indian Army officer proved to be very far from the truth. Unbeknown to us, his lack of responsibility and reliability caused huge problems for Alison throughout our childhood; often she had to hold the family together single-handedly while not knowing where the next penny was coming from. At times she could be quite short and, in the account of her life that follows, she expresses regret about her temper, but considering the stress she must have been under, it seems amazing that she was able to function at all on this knife-edge between stability and disaster. With us in tow, she was forced to move rented accommodation on average every year for seventeen years. So after Alec's sacking from the F.O., she must have felt that nothing worse could follow, but she was wrong. 'I was responsible for a two-year-old child and seven months pregnant with another. I had no money and nowhere to go. But far, far worse than the fear of my material predicament were the implications regarding A., too horrible to acknowledge.' However she was devoted to our father, and loved him unreservedly throughout his life. She stuck with him through thick and thin, beyond a level of tolerance that few would countenance these days.

From our perspective, Alexander was a loving, caring and concerned parent, and together they instilled strong principles in us, with great emphasis on courtesy and good manners, integrity and conscientiousness in all we did, underpinned by firm guidance and direction in the practice of our Catholic faith, even though Alison at this stage had not converted. Sport was an important dimension of our lives and, although it was just us and our father who kicked the football around in winter, our mother joined us for cricket games in the park, bowling and strapping on the pads and batting in her turn with a considerable level of competence acquired at Wycombe Abbey.

Alexander died on 4th April 1963, and the impact on Nigel – who was still at school and living at home – was huge. Nigel was playing in the later stages of the prestigious schools seven-a-side tournament at Rosslyn Park that day, and was amazed to see our father turn up, as he had not given any indication that he would be there. It was the last time he would ever see him. Subsequently, he treasured this opportunity he had been given to have that last conversation with Alec, which meant so much to him. In the aftermath of this tragedy he was thrown together with our mother, who had only just come out of hospital herself, having suffered a severe infection after an operation. During this time, Alexander had written a number of loving letters to her, which became even more significant in the aftermath of his death.

For Gordon the situation was very different. He had joined the Navy in May 1960 and by the time of Alec's death he had left Dartmouth and was in the brand-new frigate, HMS *Eskimo*, conducting sea acceptance trials in the Channel. The first lieutenant broke the news to him very sympathetically and relieved him of his night watchkeeping duties, Gordon remembers feeling very unemotional, and guilty that he did not feel more distressed. However, when he thought about it later, he remembered – on his last leave – having gone for a walk with our father, who'd had to stop every few yards to catch his breath. He realised he'd been half expecting the bad news.

Once home in Ealing, Gordon was eager to provide as much support to our mother as possible, and one of the ways of doing this was to register his father's death. Gordon had quite forgotten about this when, just over forty years later, Tim Crook, our father's biographer, used the register to locate him. Tim was later to be instrumental in reuniting the families.

As he grew older, Gordon came to doubt quite a few of the claims our father had made, and he decided to go to the register of births at Somerset House two weeks after his death. What he found shocked him. The only truth of what he had been told was that Alexander had been born in Dover Castle, but there was nothing to link him to the dukedom of Marlborough, as he had claimed, his parents being Second Class Staff Sergeant Alexander Wilson of the Medical Staff Corps and Annie Wilson, formerly O'Toole. His names were Alexander Joseph Patrick, very different from those listed on Gordon's birth certificate. Gordon did not tell his mother about this, not wishing to add to her grief, and nor did he tell Nigel, feeling that he was too young to have his image of his father destroyed.

The funeral arrangements were bizarre, and are covered in detail in the memoir. Alison was clearly very stressed in this period, desperate to hide the truth from us both. Neither of us had ever been to a funeral before, let alone one in which a single phrase out of place might have exposed the reality of the situation. This ended the first half of Alison's life, which changed dramatically when, a few months after our father's death, she was received into the Catholic Church, with just us present. On her first Communion the next day, she declared her intention for herself: 'that I would progress in the spiritual life'. For Alec 'she had only one wish, one concern, one prayer: for his forgiveness and salvation'. Love was still there, despite everything that had happened, and she prayed for Alec every day after that.

Our lives went on as normal. Gordon returned to his ship, from which he came home for occasional weekends and a period of leave before it deployed to the Indian Ocean for a year. During his periods at home he would often go out with Alison and both were amused to be frequently taken for brother and sister. Nigel remained near at hand and, during his time in Oxford, kept in close contact with our mother, initially very worried about the state of her mind after the death. She describes in the first part of her memoir 'a crushing burden . . . a sadness that seeped into every part of my being. There was no one with whom to share my grief.' Alison continued to support Nigel through university, including an extra year at Oxford doing a Dip. Ed., giving him the time to win his rugby blue, in front of a full house including Gordon and our mother, at Twickenham.

Through a friend, Alison was introduced to Father Corr, co-founder of the Servite Secular Institute and, according to that friend, 'a pied piper of souls'. Alison eventually came to the firm conclusion that joining the institute was God's will, and she took her first vows in August 1967. As Nigel was graduating from university in 1968, Alison was taking the final steps in leaving her past behind – giving up her job, selling the house, journeying into the complete unknown of studying Catholic theology for the Licentiate in Sacred Theology (S.T.L.) at the Jesuit College at Heythrop. From that time on, our mother confounded herself and everyone around her by the way she took on challenges that she would formerly have considered impossible – the will, she felt, was provided by the Holy Spirit. She was the first laywoman to enter the field of Catholic theology in England; she completed five years of study and gained two degrees, and later set up her own course on Christian mysticism, eventually becoming a real expert in all forms of religious mysticism. From the time she took a vow of poverty, she never had to worry about money; there was always enough support for her from charities and other fellow Catholics.

Having encouraged her to study for the S.T.L., Nigel attempted to fill the role as her guardian by listening to her and trying to reduce her stress. One of the final steps our mother took in leaving her past behind was to sell her house. In the memoir, Alison herself describes the serious dilemma she felt at this stage: she needed to push on along the path she had designed for herself, but that sense of need was countered by a real concern about how Nigel would cope with the loss of his domestic base. Both recall the awful symbolism of Nigel's disappearing down the escalator of the tube station to which she had taken him, waving good-bye to her.

So how did we feel when the revelations about our parents' lives were uncovered? We both remember feeling stunned, but above all we felt huge waves of compassion towards Alison for all she had suffered. We appreciated how hard it must have been for her to have carried all those secrets throughout her life, and realised what a relief it must have been to unburden herself and tell us the truth after so long. More complex feelings of betrayal, shock or anger towards our father, and admiration and gratitude for our mother, gradually emerged during the following months and years.

It was only after Alison's death, aged eighty-four, that the second half of her story was revealed in what she called 'After'. Because of the passion and detail with which she expresses herself in that testimony, no further words here are needed – suffice it to say that our mother saw the second half of her life as the inevitable outcome of the first, that 'Before' inexorably led to 'After', and that her life thus came full circle and with complete fulfilment.

Those who knew Alison in the latter half of her life would remember her as quiet, modest and a caring but firm grandmother, and a loyal and valued friend to many. She never drew attention to herself, and rarely voiced strong opinions, but nonetheless navigated life with serene dignity, compassion and wisdom, as well as an infectious sense of fun. Only a very few knew the depths of passion, pain and sorrow that she had experienced earlier in her life, or the intensity of her spiritual life which followed. She suffered a whole stream of illnesses with great fortitude, seeming to treat them all as a kind of penance or purgatory on earth. Despite these, her overall physical health was not bad, and once she had recovered from a hip replacement she was still very active in getting around independently. She was often busy for eighteen hours a day, and remained a wonderful guide, rock and friend for Gordon, Mary and Nigel.

She was a grandmother to eight children and great-grandmother to six; she particularly took to the latter role like a duck to water. There is a lovely photograph of her with each of Gordon's first two grandchildren, born within two months of each other, sitting on each knee. It was so appropriate that – several years later – the last picture ever taken of her was an equally precious photograph, featuring Nigel's first grandchild, a boy, sitting on her knee a day or two after his birth.

At the end, when she had to have a major operation, she was well prepared. 'I know the end; He is the end; and I know Him and have "seen" Him.' We later learned that she had told her parish priest: 'If called, I am ready to go.' In the period before her final operation, she had appeared to be as well as she had been for a long time – mentally and physically fit and very lively. When Nigel left our mother in the hospital ward on the late afternoon of 1st August to travel to Matlock for the preparations for his second son's wedding, he turned back three times wondering whether he should return and tell her that he loved her – but he did not because he did not want her to think it was more than saying good-bye. Gordon had a similar experience the next day, when they were joined for a while by a Catholic priest who said some prayers in a very fulfilling mini service, although she could not receive Holy Communion as she'd had a tracheotomy. Before he left our mother had a look in a mirror and expressed concern that her face did not look too good as a consequence of her operation. Gordon reassured her, but wished that he had gone back to emphasise strongly that in a few days it would be back to normal. However, she knew that she was loved and, to her, death was a release, a reward and a fulfilment; we felt that she had decided that it was time for her to go. She died in the very early hours of the following morning.

It was very important that Alison's gravestone should be special and fitting, and so the family chose, from a stone-mason in Norfolk, a large tablet of Cumberland Green sandstone, with just her name, and an inscription 'Thy Will Be Done'. She is buried in Addlestone Cemetery, near the little house where she lived in great contentment during her last few years.

There are just two minor errors in the text of her memoirs, which is amazing since she burned all her diaries after 1940 and it is all drawn from her memory. She stated that it was a 'buzz bomb' (V-1) that hit her hostel in 1941 (page 26), but these weapons did not enter service until 1944. It is more likely that it was an inert bomb that did its damage by pure momentum: had it exploded we would not be reading this history. Later, she mentions the West Middlesex Hospital (page 48), but this should have been the Central Middlesex: Gordon vividly remembers occasionally visiting Alexander there as a schoolboy.

Prologue

This is the true story of my life. It is true as preserved in my memory and as it reflects my attitude. However, allowance has to be made for the fact that it is over forty years since it all began and over twenty years since the sledge-hammer shock of God's gentle coming. The only records are my 1939/40 diaries and letters written to my spiritual director after 1963, and in the second part I have quoted quite extensively from the latter, as they often give a more vivid and accurate account of events and my reactions than memory can provide so many years later. Chronological exactitude cannot be guaranteed. Moreover, memory plays tricks, retaining and erasing seemingly at random, in one instance, as one of the letters showed, even entirely obliterating evidence of one of the most traumatic incidents which I would have expected to remain etched there for ever. What has been captured are those events which stand out as high and low points, great heights and great depths which I have been privileged to experience. All life, for all of us, no matter who we are, is a learning to love. Love is our driving force and it is by love and its correlate suffering that we are moulded. This story of my life is, then, a love story. Loving is the essential element which I have isolated, leaving out all the rest as being of secondary importance.

The spur which finally goaded me into action was my daughter-in-law's question: 'Why bring God into everything?' This account is the answer, which I hope will enable her to understand. I have tried to relate the facts as briefly and concisely as possible with no literary embellishment. The first part is, therefore, recorded in stark simplicity; the second has proved more difficult, requiring a certain amount of labour to grasp the ungraspable, describe the intangible. The first part is written for and belongs to my sons, who lived and held fast to their faith long before their errant mother at last entered the fold. They were for me the first and most incisive example of the faith lived, in whom there was much to emulate. Now, as I look back, I see how throughout their childhood and formative years they were overshadowed and protected by God's grace. It is as if they walked unscathed through a minefield. At any time a slight alteration in the combination of events and circumstances could have exposed the whole disastrous situation, shattering their lives and the stability of home and background. Nevertheless, they must have many questions they have patiently refrained from asking. That same faith and grace will now enable them to accept the unpalatable truth which is the answer.

The second part is for God, written in homage, adoration and thanksgiving. It belongs to his Church. Neither part is complete without the other.

Apart from my director, to whom all the facts of both parts were confided in full, I have never felt any urge to disclose anything about the wonders of God's intervention, and none of it has previously been revealed. Certain facts about the first part have been disclosed, where necessary, to make the situation clear to certain authorities. I have never confided in any friend or relative. The instinct of love is to shield rather than reveal. Yet I have always known that ultimately the whole story must be recorded in witness to the victorious power of grace and in homage and thanksgiving to the God who loves and pursues us through all the sinful episodes of our life in order that he may give himself to us totally in everlasting love.

There are, then, two parts to my life: 'Before' and 'After'; before God's coming and after God's coming. The two parts are as completely and cleanly separated by this coming as if they had been severed by a guillotine. Yet it is one life, and neither part can be fully understood except in the light of the other. Both parts are extraordinary, 'Before' on the natural level, 'After' on the supernatural.

The reading of 'Before' will be painful, distressingly so to those immediately concerned, but – where sin increases, grace abounds all the more.

'Before' is a tragedy, but it was not the end, only the beginning: a dark night, whose dawn was the tender touch of God, whose light perpetual joy. In the instant of his coming, the grief of the past was transformed into the joy of the present; the past was as if it had never been. 'After' could not keep his feet upon the ground, such joy his heart had found.

Do not grieve over the story of 'Before'; it is only the prelude. 'After' follows.

BEFORE

Chapter 1

> O God, unloose these cursèd bonds and chains,
> Set free the captive force within my mind,
> So then my yearning soul may reach the stars
> And bring to earth the dust of eternity;
> Let fall the cross of grief upon my heart,
> And then shall wake a stirring, throbbing anguish.
> Known, but only half revealed to man
> To find expression through this hand of thine.

I was nineteen when I wrote those lines. God answered my prayer, as always in a manner beyond our power to conceive – in full measure and running over. Now, nearly fifty years later, it is time for me to undertake my part: to record the history of that grief for which I had prayed, which was abundantly given and which, in fact, heralded God's coming; to pay homage to the marvels of God's work in my life.

At nineteen I was a romantic, immersed in books, poetry, dabbling on the edges of philosophy, dreaming of beauty, truth, goodness and, above all, love – but only real love would do – eternal, unbreakable, prepared to suffer all the anguish without which love would not be love. My mother was an inveterate reader, consuming novels from the nearest Boots and Smith's libraries at an amazing pace. From her and my father, whose relaxation was to shut himself up in

3

his study with the Greek and Latin classics, I inherited a love of reading. However, I followed my mother rather than my father, going for the better novels, Brett Young, Walpole, Charles Morgan, Claude Houghton, L. H. Myers, Ernest Raymond being my favourites. I read avidly, curled up in a chair, lost to my surroundings; the world of poetry and fiction with its incipient philosophy was much more inspiring and engrossing than the material world. At that time my greatest delight was to shut myself in the drawing-room, where I would be sure of solitude, put a record on the gramophone, Handel's Largo, Ketelbey's 'Monastery Garden', Richard Crook singing 'I'll Walk Beside You' or, when I had acquired it, Tchaikovsky's 5th Symphony, spread myself out on the settee and dream my dreams.

Except for three years at my first boarding school, my childhood was very happy and serene. Yet I was a solitary and very withdrawn child. My parents were old, my father in his fifties and my mother turned forty, when I was born. My father would not allow my brother and myself to have any formal schooling until we were seven, although prior to that we had some lessons from a governess. In complete opposition to today's practice, he thought the child's mind should lie fallow in the early years. At seven my brother was sent away to a preparatory school and I had two years of solitary freedom. Just as later I was able to transport myself into a fictional realm, so as a child I transported myself into the realm of imagination.

I had one great grief, which was that I had been born a girl and not a boy. The result of my parents having married so late and their first child being still-born was that when my brother arrived, after another very difficult birth, he was doted upon. I was not intended, since my mother was not supposed to have any more children. Nevertheless, I was very much loved and welcomed. However, that knowledge could not annul what rubbed off from their attitude towards

4

my brother. It was made quite clear to me that the eldest and boys had privileges which the younger offspring and, worse, girls, could never hope to acquire. I desperately wanted to be a boy and I would spend days and weeks role-playing male parts. All my games and toys were boys'. Long before it was an accepted thing, I insisted on dressing in boys' clothes, wearing my brother's shorts and dressing up in his discarded school suits, caps, cricket flannels, whatever I could lay my hands on. I would select one of his school friends and for weeks, in imagination, step into his shoes and become him. In the garden at home, dressed in the school uniform, I would play happily for hours, completely entering into my role. I would take the name of the boy I had chosen, write it on my books, 'be' him. In the holidays I played cricket with my brother on the lawn, frequently breaking the greenhouse windows, and in the winter football in the back yard. Whatever he did, I did.

Although so introvert, I was not entirely friendless. There were one or two children who could be reached by bus or bicycle with whom I was allowed to play. One, David, a vicar's son, was a much loved childhood companion, until to my sorrow, his father moved to another living. In the neighbouring house, across a field, there was a family with four undisciplined, riotous boys with whom I was strictly forbidden to play. They caused a mild form of havoc in the neighbourhood and any damage was traceable to them. I was often sent to the farm, five minutes' walk away, to fetch cream, which I would carry back in the jug without any danger of spilling; it was so thick you could turn the jug upside down. On one occasion I met the eldest of the next door boys. Whether he taunted me, I don't know, but an altercation took place and the stones started to fly, one of my stones hitting him on the temple. This, not surprisingly, resulted in a visit from an angry parent and a considerable amount of discord as each parent defended their offspring.

5

Although I had hit him, the accusation was that he had been the first to throw a stone. This I affirmed and stoutly maintained but, looking back through the mists of time, I would not like to take an oath on it now. I think my father was secretly delighted that my feminine aim had been better than my male opponent's, but the incident did not improve the already strained relations between the families. Not long afterwards tragedy hit them. The youngest boy, during one of their escapades, badly bruised his leg and shortly after died of an embolism. A spruced-up horse and cart from the farm carried the pathetic little coffin to its resting place in the churchyard a mile away. Differences were forgotten in mutual sorrow and compassion.

When I was seven I was allowed to share a governess with the vicar's children and one or two others. This meant a bicycle ride of a mile or so to the village where the classes were held above the smithy. To get there I had to pass the village school. No doubt the children resented my different status in having private lessons and not mixing with them, because when I returned home during their lunch-time play period often they would line the walls on to the road jeering at me as I rode past and, on at least one occasion, stoning me. I used to ride past as quickly as I could.

Lying was nipped in the bud quite early. I remember, at about five or six years old, going into the cold, slate-slabbed larder at Christmas time and seeing about two dozen mince pies laid out on racks to cool. Too tempting to be resisted I was afraid to help myself to one, being sure it was known exactly how many were there and that it would be missed, So, instead, I took a small bite out of each one, turning the missing portion to the wall, so that it would not be immediately evident to anyone entering the larder. When it was discovered, as the first suspect, I was questioned, but firmly denied any knowledge of it. Suspicion was then, no doubt to my relief, diverted to mice, until it was realised that no mouse was ever so symmetrical in its thieving. The full tide of censure then broke upon me. I was despatched to my room in utter disgrace, deprived of my meal and made to understand that the enormity of the offence was not the thieving but the lying about it when challenged. After that, and with the emphasis on honour at school, truth became almost a fetish.

The ethos of girls' public schools in England is very much that of the boys' schools, which means a very high moral standard. Only looking back as a Catholic did I realise the self-centred nature of this morality with its emphasis on honour. In both boarding schools I attended, lying or thieving were so rare as to necessitate the whole school being assembled and a demand made for the culprit to own up, which she usually did. The cardinal sin was not the offence against God or against another person, but the besmirching of one's own honour. Any lie or dishonourable act was a blot which, in the absence of the sacrament of penance, there was no means of erasing. I remember tears springing to my eyes when, at my first school, forbidden lemonade powder having been found in my dormitory drawer, I was told it was dishonest. I could happily break a rule, but was devastated to be charged with dishonesty. Then I could not see the connection, now I can detect the subtle way in which we were manipulated by means of honour as an all-embracing concept. Certainly the result was a reverence for truth. All through my life, even when I found myself forced to live a lie, I revered truth and, rather than make a statement, the truth of which I was not sure, would remain silent. I knew, and had been told at college, that I had a certain talent for writing, but I could only write truth. Something always held me back, prevented me from writing fiction. To do so would, for me, have been a prostitution of the talent I knew I had been given and sooner or later had to fulfil. The result is the few things I have written, including poetry, remain as true today as the day they were written – because they were written in truth. When God entered my life, I realised why I had always had this strong instinct that truth must be preserved: any account of God's workings in a human soul demands the most scrupulous honesty if distortion is to be avoided.

Unconsciously I learned to commune with nature. My bedroom window overlooked Scafell over which, if I looked out early enough, I would see the sun rise. On the other side of the house, just over a mile away, was the sea, where the sunsets were said still to be particularly impressive because of the effects of the eruption of . . .* All the countryside was mine through which to wander at will: across the fields towards the distant mountains or down through the rabbit warren, the sedge and the sandhills to the shore, where the receding tide left an isolated expanse of sand interspersed only with pebbles and rocky pools. Seldom was there another person in sight and, if I did meet anyone, I used to turn quickly and go back or, in the fields, hide behind a hedge, to avoid having to speak. I was extraordinarily and painfully shy. To talk for the sake of talking or out of politeness seemed stupid to me. At my first boarding school we used to move one place round the table every day until our turn came to sit next to the teacher at the head of the table, to whom we were supposed to 'make conversation', the burden being on us. To me this was untold and indescribable agony. I could never think of anything to say, and what did come into my head I dismissed as being too stupid or trite to merit saying. Probably because of nervous tension generated by my shyness, I used to suffer from severe attacks of sickness, regularly being confined to the infirmary at school and almost invariably, when away from home, sooner or later

* Left blank in the original manuscript but assumed to be referring to the eruption of Mount Etna in November 1928.

being overcome by sickness. This inability to converse freely and easily, certainly up to the time of my marriage, was acute and was often misinterpreted as rudeness. My parents must have been chagrined to be told when I left my first school, that they had generated a mouse. Indeed, I think when I was in my teens my father almost despaired of me because of my monosyllabic replies to his enquiries as to what I had been doing or how some outing or engagement had gone.

I had an intense love and appreciation of the beauty of nature, particularly the hills which seemed to be a part of my very being. If we went out in the car I would gaze upon and silently imbibe the almost intolerable beauty of the Cumbrian scenery, with its ever-changing kaleidoscope as the clouds hung like puffs of smoke or wads of cotton wool, gathered threateningly, blotting out the peaks, or chased each other as they raced across the sky. No two days are ever alike. The patterns created by sun and cloud, light and shadow, are infinite. Greens, blues, browns and mauves blend in ever-changing proportions with the seasons, the days, the hours. The same mountain view is never the same. Later, returning at the end of term from school in the south of England, I used to stand at the window in the train corridor, waiting with eager longing for the first glimpse of the distant outline of the hills. I was intoxicated with beauty – the beauty of nature surrounding me more than anything else, but also the beauty of words and ideas in poetry and literature, large extracts of which I used to copy into numerous notebooks, the beauty of classical music which, at nineteen, I was just beginning to be able to appreciate. I lived an intense inner life and found it difficult to relate to all but a few of my peers and a few select adults.

I related to animals, all of which I loved, more easily than to humans; they were my friends. The patient, sweet-natured, old black spaniel was the recipient of my confidences and tears and the one kitten kept out of each of the litters the potting-shed cat regularly produced was wrapped in a white cloth and duly baptised in the greenhouse water tub. But throughout my childhood and teenage years, horses were my greatest love. The clean smell of horseflesh mingled with the sweet smell of hay was scent to my nostrils, the creak of the leather of the saddles and the clink of bits music to my ears, the soft nuzzling of their muzzles more satisfying than any human touch. Surprisingly, my parents who sacrificed so much to send us to expensive boarding schools, never indulged my deepest and most persistent longing, to have a pony of my own. However, for years I regularly had riding lessons from stables a few miles away, and long before the horses were due, I would be standing at the window watching for them coming up the road. On wet mornings I would be torn with anxiety, watching for a break in the clouds. Would it be too wet, or would it clear up sufficiently to enable me to enjoy my hour or so of bliss? Never was I happier than when perched on the back of a horse, be it a sleek hunter or a weary old carthorse; as I wandered through the fields, I would climb on to the back of any horse which would stand still long enough to allow me to do so. Without any doubt, for me, horses were the most beautiful of God's creatures and I loved everything about them.

At ten I was sent to my first boarding school, but not until I was taken away three years later did I realise how unhappy I had been: a timid, wild animal, caged, deprived of the glorious freedom to which I had been used. Although my father was a solicitor, he had selected a school which was primarily for daughters of the clergy. The headmistress who, as was customary, was a D.D., preached very good sermons. The moral tone was good, but the discipline and oversight were oppressive; there was no respite from the eagle eye of an ever-present teacher. Motion along the corridor was by crocodile and, when necessary to branch to right or left, a 'square corner' had to be turned by swinging round on one foot in order to advance at an exact right angle, each person pivoting on the same spot when their part of the crocodile reached it. Naturally, the religious side was a high priority. I remember the sound of church bells on Sundays, attendance at the nearby Anglican church, fish on Fridays and seemingly endless litanies during Lent, when we had to remain on our knees on the bare boards for up to forty-five minutes. Needless to say, there were frequent casualties, sometimes one after another being carried out in a faint. A very good Christian, and particularly scriptural foundation, was provided with an on-going programme of four scripture classes every week. Homesick and, being an exceptionally light sleeper, unable to sleep in a dormitory because of the snoring and coughing of innumerable neighbours, I used to lie awake long after all the others were asleep, becoming so tired that I would work myself into a frenzy of irritation and tears of resentment that only I was still awake. One night when I was particularly unhappy, I thought I saw three shining white figures above my bed, which I hoped were angels, but which could well have been merely the product of an over-active imagination assimilating the account of the Transfiguration. Nevertheless, it was an occasion of peace and happiness.

At this time I realised the cost of true discipleship of Christ. Inevitably I looked at my parents and realised that, though they were good, indeed my father very good indeed, there was still much to be desired as regards Christian perfection. Perhaps for a little while I tried to live up to the demands of a God who was even more watchful than the school staff, whose all-seeing eye, so it was instilled into us, took account of everything. I had a friend who wanted to be a missionary, which struck me as most desirable and commendable. In those days there was still a certain glamour attached to the missions. Indeed, as far as the Church of

11

England was concerned, missionaries, and to a lesser extent the impoverished clergy, were those who did, in fact, renounce their worldly possessions in order to follow Christ. I thought that I, too, would like to surrender all and do the same. However, when I told my mother it evoked an exhortation on the perils of religious mania. My ardour cooled and I resigned myself to compromise and mediocre discipleship.

For as long as I can remember, God was always there, in the background. I never doubted his existence. However, his presence in my life followed a very ordinary and unspectacular pattern and there was no attraction to prayer, a few daily prayers hurriedly recited being the best I could do. I was, however, strongly drawn to church services, and on a Sunday would happily attend early Communion, Matins and Evensong. I listened attentively and found great sustenance and intellectual stimulus in the sermons. We were fortunate that at Wycombe Abbey the headmistress was, again, a D.D. who was an accomplished preacher, but more so in that we had Dr. Mozeley, the Dean of St. Paul's, an outstanding preacher, as our chaplain. Later, when I was at college in London, I used to scan the press in order to be able to attend Matins where he, or others equally well known, were preaching. Already a strong theological attraction was beginning to manifest itself, but there was little else to feed it. Whilst throughout my education great emphasis was laid on scripture, there was little on doctrine, which was confined to some catechetical instruction from Dr. Mozeley prior to Confirmation. I remember asking him about transubstantiation and being told I could believe it or not as I liked.

My father had a very good intellect. At fourteen he had been right through Fettes and, when his own father died of diabetes in his forties, left, and as the eldest undertook responsibility for the family and his widowed mother. One of his brothers was subsequently to commit suicide and one of his sisters, after marrying and having children, one of whom became one of the first women Fellows at Cambridge, died of T.B. After leaving school, my father read law at London University, obtaining the Law Society Prize and ruining his digestion by economising on an inadequate diet. He was a quiet man, patient and gentle, a source of help to family and clients alike, very much loved and respected. My mother used to say he would have made a good monk. Although they married so late in life, the result of her having gone to keep house for him, she was his first and only love. He was very abstemious, being a non-smoker, taking a drink only rarely when we had guests and, other than an occasional business appointment, going out only very occasionally, and then only with my mother or the whole family. A home-lover, he unfailingly arrived back from his Whitehaven office by the 6.15 p.m. train. His weekends were always spent at home, gardening or repairing and servicing the car, which necessitated disappearing underneath it in the garage pit, to which I was frequently despatched to extract him at meal times. His recreation was an occasional game of golf and to take us for a day on one of the lakes. We would have a picnic lunch by the side of the lake, with bottles of Stone ginger beer for a treat, take a boat and fish for perch. I could not raise any enthusiasm for fishing. I did not like the tins of wriggling worms, nor the procedure of impaling them on the hook. Nor could I see the point of catching numerous fish, only to throw them back again since they were not particularly good to eat. Usually I stayed on the shore with my mother who, on principle, refused to go on the water, preferring to recline in a deck chair engrossed in the latest novel.

My mother was a complete contrast. With Irish blood on her mother's side and, I suspect, Jewish on her father's, she expressed herself with passionate intensity. She had a fierce

13

temper and would let fly at my father and, although I never witnessed it, I was given to understand that she had been known to hurl things at him. Yet, in spite of her outbursts, she made it absolutely clear, and it was indeed evident, that they were deeply devoted to each other. It was impossible to doubt their mutual affection. Although I had much in common with my father, an innate shyness, an intense inner life, a philosophical bent and love of literature, I was more attached to and more at ease with my mother. Passionate and voluble, what or whom she disliked, she disliked intensely and with much vituperation. But she knew how to love. She loved my father and she loved my brother and myself. She was warm and kind-hearted and easily moved to compassion. We had many happy times and much laughter. It was she who prepared me for suffering, telling me when I was quite young that I must learn to accept it, as it is the lot of every woman. A nominal Christian, she seldom went to church even when the rest of the family did. Yet I learned the Christian prayers at her knees. I suspect there were Jewish roots with which she never came to terms. Just as, on returning from school, I used to long for the first glimpse of the hills, so I used to long for my mother's welcome. My father would drive to the station to meet me, sometimes as far as Carnforth, sixty miles away, but only my mother's presence brought satisfaction. She would be waiting in the upstairs sitting-room, standing in front of the fire and, as I entered, throw open her arms to receive me. That embrace welcoming me home was the summit of happiness.

Chapter 2

When I was thirteen I was sent to Wycombe Abbey, where I spent three happy years released from petty restrictions and restored to comparative freedom. The grounds were beautiful and extensive and at summer weekends we could take a picnic out with our friends. There were tennis courts, a lake on which we could punt, and large playing fields at the top of the hill where every afternoon we played games, lacrosse in winter and cricket in summer. I came out of my shell and made friends, having one particular friend with whom I had a close affinity and whom I loved dearly. As her parents were in India, she sometimes came to stay with me in the holidays. She had Spanish blood and was dark and attractive with large brown eyes. I used to look forward to long talks in the bedroom before going to bed. On one of these visits, when it was time for bed, she lingered downstairs flirting with my brother. Beset by my first experience of real jealousy, I retired to the sanctuary of the large bathroom linen cupboard, there to weep tears of frustration and indignation at his appropriation of my friend. I was not the stuff of which leaders are made and never became a prefect or games captain but, to my great pride, I achieved my ambition of obtaining my 1st lacrosse colours and also played for the 2nd Cricket XI. Almost as much emphasis was placed on proficiency in games as in the boys' public schools. Cricket was taken very seriously, with 'slogging' and cradle practice early every morning.

I was still painfully shy. Wearing braces on top and bottom teeth made my not very good diction worse. My greatest dread was to be asked to read aloud in French or English literature classes. Having been ridiculed by a teacher, I became inhibited and developed a phobia about reading aloud which caused me great anguish and only began to be overcome when I started lecturing. My time at Wycombe was uneventfully happy. My work, satisfactory enough to gain matriculation, was never outstanding. Reading my reports now, I realise I was too slow and careful, a fault still very much in evidence when I am preparing lectures: reluctant to being forced to admit ignorance, and with too little confidence in my own ability, I spend too much time making notes on subsidiary issues which might arise.

Keeping us both at public schools had been a strain on my father's very modest income and so I was taken away before going into the Upper Sixth. A late developer, I left school just at the point when my intellect was beginning to expand and I would most have benefited. There was nothing I would rather have done than to have gone to university to read literature or philosophy and, had I shown a strong desire to do so, I am sure, although my brother was already reading medicine at Cambridge, my father would have made even more sacrifices to make it possible. However, previously warned by my mother of the strain it would impose, when my father asked me if I wanted to go to university, I replied in the negative. It was certainly a sacrifice, because all my inclinations were in that direction, but renunciation seemed quite natural and the only possible response in the circumstances. My mother was always clever at manipulating me to accept uncomplainingly the lesser role and the lesser lot than that of my brother. Her appeal to my better nature would have the desired effect, but no doubt it also created an opening for a streak of smug self-satisfaction. I put the matter of university right out of my mind and thought no more about it until, thirty-two years later when I went to Heythrop, I marvelled how what had been sacrificed had been given back to me, in full measure and running over.

Since I was not going to university, I was kept at home for about two years, during which time I underwent a very minor sort of 'coming out' process, attending whatever was going on, which did not amount to much more than tennis parties, gymkhanas, country-house dances and the odd hunt ball, often sixty miles away in Carlisle. I was still as shy and ill at ease as ever. Dancing with the elderly host on one occasion, I was unable to think of a single comment to make until just before the music stopped, when I achieved a remark. His shattering response was, 'So you have managed to think of something to say at last!' How absurd it all seems now, but how devastating at the time. I suppose it was hoped that I would make a suitable match, but my world of inner romance materialised no further than the drawing-room couch where I dreamed my dreams. Two girls from Austria, one after the other, came to live with us on an exchange basis, the intention being that I should go and stay with them in Vienna. However, the second hurried back to vote for Hitler and the Anschluss and, needless to say, my visits never transpired. The approaching year, 1939, was indeed to be eventful.

On 1st January I arrived in London accompanied by my mother. My mini 'coming out' period unsuccessfully concluded, it had been decided that I should go to a high-powered secretarial college just off Piccadilly. The necessary arrangements and inevitable shopping completed, when term started, my mother returned to Cumberland and I was left to savour my first taste of independence, living in the college hostel. I quickly made friends, delighting in those with a more intellectual bent. From my diary, it seems I led a very full life, often going out with them to the cinema,

17

theatre, exhibitions, dances, restaurants and, as always, on Sundays pursuing the more eminent preachers. The names of many young men, some from Cumberland, others whom I met in London or who were my brother's Cambridge friends, cross the pages of the large diaries I kept during 1939 and 1940.

Several of these I found attractive and would gladly have deepened an acquaintance which they made no attempt to pursue; they must have found me hard going and very dull. Those that were persistent were always the wrong ones, the oddities. However, the trail of unrequited attractions does not seem to have marred my enjoyment, for in February I wrote, 'I _love_ life. I enjoy it all. The work, the tests. Even the things that I hate, I enjoy when taken as a whole. Without the nasty things there would be no life'; and, in March, 'I am so happy. I adore college. I have many friends and I love it. I am in love with life.' Nevertheless, I was longing for a real soul-mate: 'I long for a friend to whom I can speak of the things such as I write, but I have no such friend and therefore I must write instead. I search for the soul that each person has within them, but I am disappointed because hardly ever can I find it . . . I find myself increasingly separated from others. The more I read, the more lonely and apart I seem to become. I don't understand many people and they don't understand me. Our tastes are different. At college I am most like the others, because then I cast away all my books and concentrate solely on the work – I feel part of my friends then. I laugh and play with them – but in the hostel, no. I prefer to retire to my room and read. Though always I long for someone to talk to – to really talk to. I want to find the soul behind the outward mask.'

In the summer vacation a college friend asked me to spend August with her family in Northern Ireland, and there I was introduced to a much more lively and uninhibited social group than the staid Cumbrian society to which

18

I had been used. It was, of course, a Protestant environment and there, for the first time, I encountered anti-Catholic bigotry. Anti-Catholicism at home had never gone beyond designating the chicken's tail the 'pope's nose'. The only Catholic church was ten miles away, and sometimes on a Sunday when we were on the way to a day on the lakes, we would pass the one and only Catholic family going in the opposite direction on their way to Mass. That was the total extent of my knowledge of Catholicism; it was known to exist, but only as a rather odd kind of non-conformism which it would never have occurred to one to investigate. One of the Irish group was a young lawyer, a generation older than we were. He was handsome, vivacious and, I was told, given to bouts of drinking, on account of which I was warned against him. He too was a dreamer and we found we had much in common. He paid me a great deal of attention and was eager to meet us at the local Palais, not approved of by my friend's parents and where unbeknown to them we sometimes spent our evenings. Inevitably irre-sponsible, he twice failed to keep a promised appointment, reappearing very contrite some days later. I was completely captivated by him but, although ignorant of the effects of drink, was very aware of this undesirable side of his char-acter and would have relished the opportunity of reform-ing him. Of course reconciliation fanned the coolness resulting from his misdemeanours into renewed ardour. One beautiful moonlight night we sat on a seat overlooking the sea at Portrush. It was the perfect romantic setting. He took me in his arms and gave me my first kiss. It had no effect whatsoever; I was still unawakened. I never saw him drunk and he respected and reverenced my innocence. It was towards the end of August – the political situation was worsening rapidly, and within a few days a telegram had summoned me home. He drove me to Belfast and we bade each other a fond farewell on the boat, intending to meet when he visited London. I never saw him again. I arrived home just in time to hear Chamberlain's announcement that we were at war, which disposed of our plans for reunion. I wrote him very long letters every few months, to which he replied at somewhat less length. Absence made the heart grow fonder and, although I never revealed it to him, he held first place until, the war at its height, I met A.* and the correspondence died a natural death. I often wondered what had happened to him.

I suppose, due to the uncertainty of what was going to happen once war had been declared, I was again kept at home. However, as things remained quiet, it was decided, probably thinking more opportunities could be created for finding my brother and myself suitable partners, to move the family to London for a year. A house was rented in Roehampton, close to the gates of Richmond Park. We left Cumberland at 1.30 a.m. on the morning of 7th December, my brother driving the larger car, whilst I followed in the smaller one. It took us eighteen hours to get to London. Before we left Cumberland, I had skidded and just managed to keep the car out of the hedge. Round about Preston, at 6.30 a.m., we ran into thick fog and had to creep at 10 m.p.h. for an hour or more, stopping for breakfast at 8.30 a.m. For the rest of the journey there was ice on the road. In one place we passed eight lorries and one car smashed up through skidding, and in another an aeroplane had crashed by the road. Twelve lorries crashed at Dunstable alone that morning. We were so late there was no time to stop for lunch. About St. Albans we ran into fog again, by which time it was nearly dark, and again had to reduce our speed to 10 m.p.h. At Mill Hill we decided to abandon the smaller car and all go on in the larger, not daring to risk losing each other in the fog and dark, finally arriving at Roehampton at

* Alexander Wilson.

7.30 p.m. My diary states: 'I would never go through it again ... the strain was almost unbearable and the risk wicked. We could see neither road nor pedestrians, nor stationary cars. It was a gamble with death the whole way.'

During the seven months we were at Roehampton, there were various young men, with whom I rode in the park or who took me to dances or the theatre, but still no serious or lasting relationship evolved. One, a Captain in the Army, a brother of one of my friends, worked fast. He had to. Time closed in upon our generation; we were very conscious of its shortness and the unpredictability of the future. He took me out for the evening and, coming back in the taxi, kissed me and told me he loved me. 'How ridiculous,' I thought, 'he has only known me a few hours.' I was beginning to gain an insight into the ways of men, but not sufficient to stand me in good stead.

Now that I was back in London, I returned to college for a month to complete my course, and find a job. Several I turned down as they were only offering £2 a week. With a combination of the right contacts and the right strings being pulled, I found myself accepted by the Foreign Office at the princely sum of £3.5.0 per week with 5/- extra for late nights. The day came (1st April 1940) when, after being carefully vetted and having signed the Official Secrets Act, I went along to a well-known and seemingly banal branch of the F.O. near St. James's Park, but which proved to be a camouflage for more intriguing activities. The head of the department to which I was to belong was a very masculine woman. She was short, unattractive, very tubby, a chain smoker with heavily stained fingers who, when amused, chuckled rather than laughed, and who was, I am sure, very efficient at her job, having ten to fifteen men and three secretaries under her direct control. She took me up a narrow back staircase and, as we ascended, I had a strong sensation of walking towards my fate, which indeed was the case. At the top of the stairs we were confronted with a locked door, which she opened with her keys. On entering I saw that we were in what looked like a vast telephone exchange. A mechanic was working in an area where there were rows and rows of wires and plugs, whilst all round the large room were men seated at desks, each wearing earphones, manipulating a receiving instrument on his desk and obviously taking down what he heard. I was in that section of the S.S. [Secret Service], as it was then known, which was responsible for the phone tapping of all the embassies and consulates in London. Each operator was an expert in several languages.

One of these was a middle-aged man, whose dark hair was beginning to thin and turn grey, whom the others seemed to like and respect and whom they nicknamed Buddha because of his supposed wisdom. I learned that he was a Major in the Indian Army and, what intrigued me far more, that he was a writer. The languages he claimed were about five, including Arabic, Persian, Hindustani and Chinese. At first I seem to have been more interested in another member of the staff, but quite soon my attention had shifted to A.

The first air-raid warning came on 24th June at 1 a.m., when we dressed, took our gas masks, went downstairs and made cups of tea; then, since nothing was happening, went back to bed. The all-clear went three hours later. By August the raids had started in earnest and on the 25th a bomb was dropped nearby at Barnes, killing four people. Two nights later there was a six-hour raid, during which we joined our neighbours in their shelter, spending a cramped and sleepless night. The guns in Richmond Park were firing salvos which made the shelter vibrate and could be heard whizzing overhead. Not surprisingly my mother and father decided it was time to retreat and on 9th September they departed for Cumberland, leaving me installed in a hostel in Harrington Gardens.

(Unfortunately, after A.'s death, because of the queries which would have been raised and the distress caused had I not written this account, I destroyed all records from the point where my association with him began and removed the remaining pages from my 1940 diary. From now on, therefore, I have to rely on memory alone.)

Because of the frequent air raids in 1940, when we were on duty at the F.O. we were able to eat in the canteen and sleep on the floor in the basement. The staff, therefore, spent a considerable amount of time together. Quite soon there was mutual interest between A. and myself. He asked me to dine with him at the Authors' Club, nearby on the Embankment, of which he was a member and there, and sometimes elsewhere, we had many meals together. He had had several spy stories published, the Wallace books under his own name and others under more than one pseudonym. He made no secret of the fact that he was married, with a son, aged about ten, and that he was in the process of a divorce, his wife having walked out on him. He usually wore uniform, that of the 1/8th Punjabis. We would return late at night in the darkened streets, often having to run for cover from the shrapnel as it bounced round us on the street. The relationship developed but, deeply in love though I was, I would have been content to step out of the picture had there been any hope of his wife returning. Indeed, the inevitable pain would bear witness to the reality of love. However, he assured me that there was no such possibility, that she had taken the child and returned to her parents in Yorkshire and that the divorce was grinding through its slow process. Presently he asked me to marry him as soon as the divorce was through. He was patient and never rushed anything. He taught me to love. He taught me the meaning of love by the depth of his demand; he was prepared to wait until I was able to commit myself irrevocably to a self-gift that went far beyond the sexual.

One great problem that had to be overcome as soon as I realised I wanted to marry A. was his introduction and acceptance by my family. Purporting to be twenty years older than me, but in fact twenty-seven years older, in the process of a divorce and of somewhat obscure background, with no home other than furnished accommodation to offer, he was hardly an ideal suitor, and it was nothing short of a miracle that my father made no difficulties. Before the end of 1940 I took him up to Cumberland to meet my parents and he seemed to be favourably accepted. He was in uniform, which gave him status, by then promoted to Lieutenant-Colonel, and it would be presumed, a reasonable income. He claimed to be a Chesney Wilson with connections with the Marlboroughs and to have a house, at Ringwood in the New Forest, which had been requisitioned and would therefore be unobtainable as a home until the end of the war. When my mother, succumbing to her streak of snobbery, resorted to Debrett's, only to find that the facts given by A. did not tally, he then 'admitted' to being the illegitimate son of an illicit love affair of a member of the Marlborough family which, of course, was unverifiable. A. had an extraordinary ability to make anyone believe anything. He was likeable, kind, gentle, quiet, abstemious, exteriorly reliable, and perhaps his great-est attraction, to me at any rate, was his apparent modesty. For instance, I learned, whether from him or his colleagues I cannot now recall, that he had been awarded the DSO and DSC 1914–18 but did not wear the ribbons on his uniform. Only at my instigation did he put them up.

It was obvious his colleagues thought him someone rather special. He maintained he was a qualified air pilot and during the early part of the war claimed to crew in bombing flights over Germany. He would disappear for a night or two, supposedly on a bombing expedition which, needless to say, caused me great anxiety. On one occasion he returned with a large, jagged wound across the top of his wrist, which

24

he said had been caused by shrapnel. Nearly always when the sirens sounded, he would take his tin hat and go out and help the wardens. On his chest he was severely scarred with what were unmistakably old shrapnel wounds from the First War; he also had a leg injury which caused a very slight limp, and claimed to have a plate inserted on one temple. The combination of the uniform and the Foreign Office employment gave an aura of respectability which, I suppose, lulled my parents' suspicions. However, my father, a solicitor and registrar of the County Court, was by no means gullible and, I later learned, started making enquiries. However, in the midst of these, in January 1941, he died suddenly, and they were never pursued.

When my father died A. was still living in the rented house in Hendon from which his wife had deserted him. Not long after he asked me to spend the weekend with him and, after much deliberation, I went. I remember that as I stood waiting for the bus to take me there, I knew exactly what I was doing: I was going against every convention with which I had been brought up; I was putting myself in a situation where, sooner or later, I would break the letter of the sixth commandment, in spirit already broken. I was associating with a married man, not yet divorced; divorce in my upbringing had been an exceptionally rare occurrence, a thing of shame not to be discussed in front of the children. What I was doing was a clear case of a fundamental option, in which I knowingly and deliberately changed the course of my life and, in doing so, turned away from God. The Devil is exceedingly subtle. It was not with my desire, not yet fanned to its full flame, but with A.'s need that he trapped me. I have always known, but been reluctant to affirm, even to myself, that his very manifest need was the deciding factor. Thus does the Devil wrap the evil deed in the guise of good. Not that weekend, but later, he completed his work.

One evening after supper I was in my room right at the top of the hostel in Harrington Gardens when the air-raid siren sounded. I took no notice; raids were by then so frequent that one became acclimatised and nonchalant. I was on my knees by my bed writing my diary, which I did at length recording my impressions, including a good deal about my relationship with A. It was the time of the buzz bombs. Provided you heard them flying overhead, you were all right, someone else was going to get it. If the noise stopped, you knew you were in for trouble; the engine had cut out and it was about to drop. That is exactly what happened. The noise stopped suddenly, there was a pause, and then a terrific crash, followed by a rumbling and shaking of the whole house, and we were plunged into total darkness. I rushed towards the door. I could not open it, it was jammed; a sickening terror overwhelmed me. I was right at the top of the house and I knew I was absolutely alone. I knew the house had been hit, and it seemed I was trapped. I tugged again violently at the door and it came open.

Out in the passage it was pitch dark and there was an eerie hush; I felt my way round the corner. Then I was met by what I thought were clouds and clouds of dense smoke – there was a hot, flinty smell of burning. Again I felt a blinding terror, because I thought that surely the stairs below me were on fire. I had one instinct: to get down those stairs, to run through flames if necessary. And so in pitch darkness and in the choking dust, I leaped down the stairs, scrambling over bricks and rubble. I had no recollection of how I got down the first three flights; suddenly I found myself scrambling over debris on the first floor. I heard voices and what sounded like someone calling for help. All I wanted was to be with someone. I tried to go in the direction of the voices, but I could not because of the debris. Then I saw a light in the hall and, rushing on down the last flight, found everyone gathered in the hall, a knot of people standing, silent, frightened and covered in white dust. I joined them trembling from head to foot.

The bomb had hit the house at an angle of 45 degrees, destroying the whole section under my room, which now jutted out right at the top of the house with a void beneath it. Entering the ground-floor dining-room, where shortly before we had all been having an evening meal, it had removed everything above except my room. Only one girl was trapped with a badly crushed leg and foot, and we stood in the hall whilst the A.R.P. men very gently carried her down. It must have been she I heard calling, and I deeply regretted not making more attempt to go to her aid, although if I had, I would almost certainly have fallen to my death or been severely injured. I felt it was a failure in time of trial, an occasion of cowardice and fear in which a primitive and all-consuming instinct for self-preservation had blotted out the power to act reasonably. Subsequently I wondered if God had been offering me a quick route to heaven. If I had been a Good Samaritan and responded to the demand of charity, I might have been shot straight into eternity. As it was, I was left to make my way in this world. I soon strayed along a wrong path and the journey back was long and hard.

We had to evacuate the hostel and I had to find other accommodation. A., who was very concerned, obtained a room for me in the boarding house in Earl's Court Road, where he was by then living, having given up the Hendon house. There, in due course, we became lovers. Before long I was pregnant.

How had I arrived at a situation which was so out of character? As I was later to find, I had been deceived. But that was only half the story; I was never coerced. What I did, I did freely, not impetuously, but after much deliberation. Only love could induce me to betray my better self. Once I had surrendered and admitted my love, I loved with an intensity which enabled me to sacrifice everything I held most dear – goodness, truth, honour – an intensity that was to survive every onslaught except that of God himself. The fact that the situation was not actually such that I had been led to believe in no way alters my responsibility for my share in the sin and guilt of a relationship which was forbidden by my conscience and by the law of God. I would have staked all I had on myself as being the last person to become involved in such a situation. This must have been quite soon after my father's death. I wondered if I would have been able to do it if he had still been alive or whether the influence of what I knew to be his exceptional morality in all spheres would have deterred me. I had greater love for my mother, but greater respect for my father, and I was grateful I never had to inflict the wound that knowledge of my conduct would have caused him.

As a Catholic, A. had to account for the fact that, even when divorced, he would not be free to marry. He told me he was trying to obtain an annulment and that when this came through we would be able to marry in a Catholic church. That was what I wanted, because then, I thought, things would be put right before God and our union would be blessed. At what point A. announced that he had obtained his divorce, I do not remember. But, although once I knew I was pregnant, I put a lot of pressure on him regarding marriage, he constantly delayed it on the grounds of waiting for the annulment to come through. Eventually he told me that that, too, had been granted. We were married in Our Lady of Victories, Kensington, on the feast of her Birthday, 8th September 1941. The church had been bombed and the basement of a store in Kensington High Street had been adapted as a temporary measure. Regulations regarding mixed marriages were still very strict, only the minimum being allowed. The ceremony was very brief, the priest seemed disinterested and only my mother and brother were present. The marriage had taken place at the high altar before the Blessed Sacrament, it had all the adjuncts of ecclesial approval, yet I knew that the blessing for which I yearned had not been given; God, most certainly present in the Tabernacle, had turned his back.

Chapter 3

I suppose the most unpleasant thing I ever had to do in my life was to tell my mother, shortly after we were married, that I was nearly six months pregnant. Once she had recovered from the shock, she rose to the occasion and accepted the situation without further recriminations. She was a good mother and, although she could pour forth a flood of indignation and vituperation when displeased or shocked, in all my difficulties she stood by me to the best of her ability. As things worsened I often had to endure a torrent of abuse of A., each word a lashing which caused me acute pain, but I do not recall that my untimely pregnancy was a prolonged issue. Shortly before being married and to ensure there would be no suspicion of my condition, I gave my notice in at the F.O., having been there just over a year. The head of the department was very opposed to the marriage and warned me against A., but I dismissed her advice.

No doubt desiring to give a good impression and to live up to expectations, A. began in a conventional manner. He gave me a pearl necklace for my twenty-first birthday, a month before we were married; it was good, beautifully graded, probably cultured. For my wedding present he gave me a diamond necklace: whether it was, in fact, diamonds, I do not know, I had no experience of such things. My engagement ring was a large sapphire surrounded by diamonds, undoubtedly genuine. The baby was born in the private wing of St. Mary's

Hospital. All this must have cost a considerable amount of money. I was no longer working or contributing in any way to the income. The birth was long and difficult, the pain intolerable, yet in this I was still subject to the conditioning of my upbringing and my inhibitions; nothing would have induced me to let out so much as a squeak. I think if it had been allowed to go on long enough, I would have died equally quietly and uncomplainingly. I remember gnawing at my arm to try to divert the pain. I said nothing, but I put the whole appeal of the agony I was feeling into my eyes, which followed the gynaecologist's every move and sought his imploringly. At last, after thirty-two hours, he succumbed to that appeal and decided to use forceps, and the blessed mask was laid upon my face, wafting me into unconsciousness. Within twenty-four hours I was gravely ill with puerperal fever; pain which should have vanished with giving birth, returned in an equally acute but new form. I was put onto M. & B.,* which had just come out, and the combination of this notoriously depressive drug with probably some postnatal depression led to a state of misery such as I have never experienced before or since. The baby was perfect, a beautiful boy with extraordinarily blue eyes and hair so fair that it was almost white, but I was too ill to experience the joy which I should have felt. I was in hospital three weeks and then came out earlier than I should as A. admitted to concern over the hospital bills.

We had been living in furnished rooms and soon moved to a furnished flat in West Hampstead. Not long after, whilst I was taking the baby for his weekly check-up at the clinic, the flat was burgled and all my jewellery, what A. had given me and what I had been given prior to my marriage and as a child, together with some of his things, was stolen. About this time A. was dismissed from the F.O. He explained it as a ruse to give an impression of discredit for S.S. purposes.

* Antibacterial medication.

Our next move was to a little furnished house in Hampstead Garden Suburb. I remember, on first entering the bedroom, being overwhelmed by a terrible sense of foreboding. I was gripped by a sickening fear that something awful was going to happen in that room. This was probably engendered by the fact that by then A. had a stomach ulcer with occasional slight haemorrhage, which frightened me. Added to which he said the hospital he attended as an outpatient had diagnosed a rare blood disease, from time to time requiring blood transfusions which necessitated an overnight stay. For several years he would disappear for twenty-four hours, saying he was going for his transfusion. All this caused me great anxiety, underpinned as it was with the more basic phobia over the difference in our ages. I was desperately afraid of his dying which, by all the laws of nature and chance, I was going to have to endure sooner or later. I associated my premonition with my habitual phobia, struggling to overcome a sickening fear that death was going to visit us there. Disaster did overtake us, but of a different kind.

Now that A. had lost his job at the F.O., our financial situation became desperate. He always maintained that he did not want me to work and that I had to look after the baby. There was virtually no money coming in and we fell behind with the rent for the furnished house. We had a woman who came a few hours a week to clean and, though I begrudged the few shillings for her wages, I could not bring myself to admit it to her and dismiss her: I was too proud to admit our penury. When the contents of the larder were reduced to little more than a packet of macaroni, she took it upon herself to go. A. was out most of the time, walking the streets searching for work and for less expensive accommodation. One day I returned from a meagre shopping expedition pushing the pram containing G.,* who must have been a year or eighteen

* Gordon Wilson, born 20th January 1942.

months, to find myself locked out of the house. Because of the arrears of rent, the owners had taken possession and evicted us. There was nowhere to go, we had no friends or acquaintances in the vicinity. Indignant at the cruel treatment and deeply humiliated, I sat in the garden, with G. still in the pram, for I don't know how many hours until A. returned. As far as I recall, we did not have access to any of our belongings. The outcome was that the local Anglican vicar, to his everlasting credit, took us in and sheltered us for two nights, by which time A. had managed to find accommodation for us in a boarding house in Paddington. My shame at the whole course of events was overwhelming.

The Paddington boarding house was not as sleazy as one might expect. The occupants were a motley collection, including an R.A.F. officer and his wife and a Pakistani doctor, with whom we sometimes played bridge in the evenings. Problems over the rent continued. I don't know where A. got what little money there was. I understood that for some months the F.O. had continued to pay him, but by then that must have ceased. One source was the pawnbroker, to whom went, one by one, items of any value which had been left from the burglary. Some small pieces of family silver which my mother had lent us went that way without my knowing at the time. Practically nothing was redeemed; there was never enough money. The landlady was a plump, Irish Catholic, never missing Sunday Mass. Her temper would rise in proportion to the arrears in rent until a major row ensued and somehow the money was found. I used to wonder how she reconciled her abusive outbursts of temper with her faith. A. borrowed money from any available source – his friends, my friends – usually without my knowledge and to my consternation if I found out. Most was never repaid. To add to our problems, I was pregnant again.

To get G. and myself away from London and the air raids and to provide a holiday, it was arranged that the two of us

34

should go and stay with an elderly relative of mine and her daughter on the outskirts of Keswick. I had often stayed with them as a child. The house was large, graciously furnished, quietly and smoothly run. It rested on the hillside with large gardens, kitchen gardens and several fields, cottages, stables and garages. My 'aunt' in her eighties could have stepped straight out of a Galsworthy or Walpole novel; her snowy, white hair piled on top of her head, she was always immaculately dressed with a white ruffle round her neck. Kind and welcoming though she was, the whole house, which she ruled with a rod of iron, revolved round her; she was someone to be respected and feared. By then they must have been informed by my mother that everything was not quite as it should be in my life, although the more sordid and shaming details would have been withheld. Nothing, of course, was said, and I was received and made to feel at home as always.

G. and I shared a bedroom. A few nights after our arrival he suddenly woke up, sat straight up in bed and started to tear at his head. A sinking gripped the pit of my stomach as I leaped out of bed to examine his head. Sure enough there were lice crawling around. Having pursued and destroyed them to the best of my ability, I discovered to my horror that I, too, had them. As a considerable amount of head washing was going to be involved, in all fairness I felt bound to tell my cousin, who duly informed her mother. Today little would be thought of the incident, which has become quite common in schools of all classes. Then it was something unheard of outside the servants' quarters. Of course war conditions provided a cover and explanation for such afflictions. It could be put down to the train journey, but I knew we had been infected in the Paddington boarding house where a somewhat disreputable old woman was contaminated.

Humiliation crawling up my spine was like the slow progress of the perpetrators of my misery. Yet I voluntarily

35

added to that humiliation: I asked to borrow £100. I had to force myself to overcome my repugnance, reinforced as it was by the conditioning of my upbringing, A. had written to say that he was desperate for money. No power on earth except love would have enabled me to do it. For love I would almost, but not quite, have sold my soul. Fortunately and wisely, although they were very wealthy, they refused. It is part of the extraordinary pattern of my life, under the guiding hand of God, that where an injustice seemed to be done to me, years later, unbeknown to the original actors in the drama, it was made good through the same sources – in full measure and running over. As the second part of the story unfolds, it will be apparent how this came about in this instance, and how the pattern of restitution constantly recurs. Of course it works the other way as well; I, too, am given opportunities, which I must recognise and in which I must cooperate, to make restitution for my sins and failings.

Prior to being married, I had not been instructed in the Catholic faith, so A. arranged for me to go once a week to the Carmelites in Kensington, merely for information and interest. At first, although usually going to Mass with A., I had continued to go to my own church at Christmas and Easter. However, once I had started to live with A., I had felt unable to receive Communion and with that it lost its hold. As my interest and knowledge of Catholicism grew, my allegiance to the Church of England waned, until it no longer had any meaning for me. Its death knell was when A. pointed out the anomaly of its origin, something which had never previously been brought home to me. One Sunday we were returning from Mass. A., as usual, was in uniform, and I was pushing G. in the pram. As we strolled happily along, two men approached A. and took him aside for a few minutes – they were arresting him for wearing uniform under false pretences.

36

I don't recall the exact sequence of events: whether they took him away there and then or whether we returned to our room with the police and the room was searched. But within a very little time he had gone and I was alone with G. It has always been part of my make-up to bear my own pain alone and silently, and in particular not to inflict adult crises on uncomprehending and innocent children. No sign must be given to G. that anything was amiss. I remember taking him down to lunch in the dining room as if nothing had happened, knowing that before long it would be a sensation echoing all over the house. The shock of what had happened was appalling; I was stunned, sick and cold with terror. What was I to do? When it became known, in view of our bad past record, the landlady would never allow me to stay on alone. I was responsible for a two-year-old child and seven months pregnant with another. I had no money and nowhere to go. But far, far worse than the fear of my material predicament were the implications regarding A., too horrible to acknowledge.

Somehow the day must have passed. I believe I did some ironing. I always iron in a crisis – I have ironed many times since in times of crisis or tension. I had a rosary, which A. had given me, but I had never said it and hardly knew how to. That night, when I was ready for bed, I knelt down and, with my prayer book as a guide, said the whole Rosary, imploring Our Lady to intercede that A. might return. I found it difficult concentrating on my intention, the mysteries and the words, as if I were being asked to do three things at once. It took me about an hour, at the end of which time I climbed miserably into bed. It was about 11 p.m. Hardly had I got into bed, than the door opened and A. walked in. He had been released, but only for the night; the following morning he had to go back for the court hearing.

He was sent to Brixton with, I later learned, two convictions to run concurrently. He was given remission for good

37

conduct and, as far as I recollect, must have served about a month or six weeks. Once a week I visited him, taking a 2 oz. tin of his favourite tobacco. The bedraggled queue, nearly all jaded women, with hopeless, anxiety-ridden faces, outside the prison gates waiting for the short visiting time to begin must, I thought, be the saddest queue in the world – and I was part of it. The cold sordidness of it frightened and repelled me.

I did not know what to expect; it was a world of which I knew nothing. The bolts clanged back and we stepped through a door in the great prison gates. There were warders everywhere, parcels had to be handed in and particulars given. I believe we sat in a cold, bare room on backless benches, waiting to be called to spend a few minutes with our errant loved one when their number was called. I remember being taken into another room up to a section of something rather like a post-office counter, screened with bars, and possibly even glass as well. Behind the bars stood A. If there was glass, as I think there was, there must have been an aperture to speak through, but I know conversation was difficult and warders were patrolling within earshot. Whether there were other conversations going on on either side, I do not recall; I was too engrossed in what I had to say and hear.

When A. had returned on the night of his arrest, I had of course questioned him. His explanation was that it was all part of an S.S. plot publicly to discredit him so that he would be able to carry out an intelligence job, the details of which he could not tell me. Throughout this was his defence. Where complications or seeming inconsistencies arose he was always able to embellish his case with further inventions, until a vast fabrication was built up. He never forgot what he said or contradicted himself. He was extremely plausible, and many others besides myself were convinced by him. He had a trump card in that he had been part of the

F.O. system; I *knew* that was true, that therefore what he said might just be true. Stranger things did happen in intelligence work, especially in time of war. To this I clung as to a lifeline. I wanted to believe him. I could not face the consequences of not believing.

I loved him because of the good I saw in him. As a husband and in the home he was good, kind, gentle, peaceful. He was a wonderful father, who adored his children, brought them up in their faith and fostered in them only the highest ideals, of which he appeared an exemplar. He was abstemious and spent hardly anything on himself: some tobacco for his pipe, an odd pint of beer and visit to a football march, taking the children when they were old enough, was his limit. He had immense courage, reinstating himself after his lapses and continuing to work to the end, in spite of severe heart trouble. The difference in our ages had, for me, never been an obstacle, other than the death-anxiety already referred to. I was happy and content to be with him. All I wanted or asked of life was to 'be together'. That made amends for any amount of hardships or difficulties. Whilst I was with him, I was happy. Because I loved him, or my concept of him, so much, I could not face not believing in him. Although I nagged him, endeavouring to be able to extract a credible structure from what he told me, I never forced the issue to an ultimate conclusion. I never attended the police courts, nor questioned any authority about him; I could not risk total disillusionment.

When, at that first visit to the prison, I raised my suspicion that there had been no divorce, almost immediately he admitted it: the other conviction he was serving was for bigamy. His wife, however, was not the mother of the ten-year-old boy who had deserted him at Hendon but the mother of three grown-up children, whom I had believed to be his sister-in-law. One thing he continued to maintain – that there *had* been an annulment of that marriage; in other words that he had deceived me over the identity, but not the facts: his real marriage to the mother of three had been annulled. This he continued to assert to his dying day and, at one point, had Rome searching for documents which he said had been lost in the war. For the only time, I saw him weep. Tears ran down his cheeks as he begged me to forgive him and not to leave him. It was a devastating shock: the other woman and family was not what I had suspected. I gave him my word. There was no alternative. I loved him and could not abandon him in his need.

As I walked away from the prison, in spite of the shock, the humiliating shame of the disclosure and the hopelessness of my predicament, I had a sense of peace, almost joy. There had been no temptation to abandon him; love had been tested and found to be true. Moreover, although I realised that morally it could be argued that, now that there was no question of being married to him, I ought to leave him, as surely as I knew I had sinned in entering into a relationship with him in the first place, I knew that in now remaining with him I was not only acting according to my conscience but was doing right in the sight of God. In loving him, I had given myself to him. I could never retract the gift, least of all at this time of his greatest need. Love, if it was indeed love, was steadfast and everlasting. Love, that is charity in the real sense of the word, although I did not think in that terminology then, demanded that I stand by him. There was no option. It was not hard, I still loved him.

My situation was now even more desperate: no money, no home, no status, a two-year-old child to look after and another due within a couple of months There was no welfare state. The whole course of events was something entirely alien to me and I had no knowledge of what to do or where to turn for help. I hoped not for material help, but for some gesture of consolation and guidance from the Carmelite to

40

whom I had been going for instruction. He must have known, because the landlady was in frequent contact with the priory and would have been unable to resist passing on such a sensational morsel. Probably he remained silent in order not to embarrass me. But I was deeply grieved that the Church had seemed to abandon me and had made no gesture of compassion towards me in my distress. It was twenty years before I resumed instruction.

There were many disasters of one kind or another in the course of our life together. I never told anyone anything about any of them, least of all my mother or brother. I always tried to hide what was happening, but usually they found out, as they did on this occasion, a friend passing on to my mother a cutting about it from one of the evening papers. There had always been a streak of snobbery in my mother. A.'s supposed rank and background had made up for his too modest income and lack of a home. The shock of the disclosure, fortunately limited to the charge of false pretences, must have been even greater for her than it was for me. Everything about it must have been anathema to her, but no more than I could renounce A. in his need, could she abandon me in my need. She came to my aid.

It was impossible for me to stay on in the Paddington boarding house; I had no money and had to get out within days. My mother was living with another woman as a paying guest and, stretching her very meagre finances to provide completely for us, she took G. and me in with them. However, first there was a problem to be overcome. My suitcase was in the custody of a pawnbroker in the Harrow Road, and I did not have sufficient money to redeem it. I did, however, still have a pair of riding boots, so I took these to exchange for the case. I remember bringing the case back on the bus and people looking with consternation at this very pregnant woman with such a huge case, not realising that it was empty.

41

I must have been with my mother about four weeks when I went into labour, a month prematurely, due no doubt to the shock. A. had been released just previously and had managed to find temporary digs for himself. There was no question of his coming to my mother's. She was prepared to shelter G. and me, but not him. She had arranged that, during the birth, G. should be sent away to a children's home in Buckinghamshire, and there A. took him, whilst I went into the Redhill Hospital at Edgware, no private wing this time.

It was not such a difficult birth as G.'s, but neither was it an easy one. My situation was in total contrast. Then everything had been that to which I was accustomed and I had experienced the status and security of a married woman with a loving husband to take all the responsibility, to visit me and to share the joy of our child. There was dignity in the whole process and my behaviour had been strengthened by and had reflected that dignity. Now I had no legitimate status, nowhere to go and no money. I was totally dependent on the charity of my mother, something which could not continue after I came out of hospital. I would leave hospital responsible not for one child only, but for two and possibly for an ex-prisoner as well. I was demoralised before I went into the labour ward, a state not helped by the conditions in the hospital. It was a busy morning and several took their turn before me, their groans and screams being clearly audible emerging from the delivery room.

In due course my turn came. They gave me a mask to put over my face to inhale when the contractions came, but I remember having to tell them that it was useless because it was not connected with the apparatus. In the delivery room I was conscious of screams which got louder and louder, until they seemed to be bouncing off the walls. Suddenly they stopped. There was silence. It was over. I saw the baby with his dark, damp hair plastered on his head – and I loved

42

him. With G., because of the operation, I had been deprived of that precious first glimpse of the cause of such intense pain, pain that vanishes at the moment new life enters the world. Then, as with the easing of the pain I looked around the delivery room with the doctor and nurses, it dawned upon me to my horror that the screams I had heard bouncing off the walls had been my screams. I had not just screamed, I had screamed with the full force of my lungs, in a rising crescendo, as each of the final contractions took hold of me, louder than any of my predecessors. I had succumbed to the grip of a primitive terror. I realised that for a little while I had been totally demoralised; I had descended to the purely animal. I had lost my human dignity – and I was overwhelmed with shame.

Because of the desperate situation, my mother and brother tried to persuade us to have the new baby adopted, but neither of us would hear of it. We called him Nigel, because he came out of so much darkness, what I hoped would be the darkest period of my life, never to be repeated. But worse was to come.

Chapter 4

Soon after I came out of hospital, we were able to get together again. A. got a job as an assistant cinema manager with one of the big cinema chains, and we went to live in Lincoln. His salary was £6 a week and our rent £2.10.0d. Until I could wean N.* on to a bottle and take part-time secretarial work, the four of us had to live on £3.10.0d. a week. Acute poverty reduces you to a state of indecision. It is so vital to get the best value for your money that you are unable to make a choice. I remember a low point when there were only a few pennies left with which to buy a meal and I walked up and down outside the greengrocers quite unable to come to a decision as to whether to buy some potatoes, which were more filling, or some carrots, which during the war were highly extolled for their vitamin value and which would have been better for the children. After a few months A. was transferred back to London, to Purley and then to Palmers Green. We were always on the move from one set of rooms to another. In seventeen years we averaged one move per year, sometimes because of A.'s job, sometimes because the landladies would not tolerate the children, sometimes because of financial or other crises.

A. retained his job and was promoted to cinema manager. For four years things went comparatively smoothly. We had

* Nigel Wilson, born 8th November 1944.

rented a furnished house and, in order to help with the rent, took in a couple as paying guests, for whom I had to cater and clean. My confidence in A. had returned and I had laboriously rebuilt my belief in him and his explanations. Then suddenly in 1948, when G. was 6 and N. 4, all was again shattered. He was in trouble again, this time with regard to some money missing at the cinema for which, as manager, he was responsible and which he maintained had been stolen. He was tried at Marylebone Police Court, convicted and served another prison sentence. At the time I was 'temping' with an agency and, strangely, had a job almost adjacent to the police station where, in my lunch hour, I went to see him in the cells after he had been convicted. As always I could not bring myself to attend the hearing. I did not have the courage to risk corroboration: I preferred the agonising uncertainty of my suspicions in which there was room for hope. Until his death I lived a constant interior battle between chilling suspicion and the sweet balm of belief. With all my heart and soul I wanted what he said to be true; I wanted him to be genuine. It was all that mattered to me, and I would grasp at any straw to lull suspicion.

Whatever was happening, however desperate the crisis, I always had to carry on as if nothing unusual were taking place. So it was. I said nothing to anyone, but just absented myself from work at lunch-time. I must have been the most unprepossessing of secretaries; sad, drab, with no money to spend on clothes, distraught with anxiety, it is no surprise that, for the one and only time in my life, I lost my job. I was dismissed, without any explanation, by the firm near the police station – maybe they knew what was going on. In any case, just then I must have been a lot less than efficient at my job. Fortunately there was no problem about another job, the agency just sent me elsewhere.

I knew then that A. could not be relied upon and that I had to take full responsibility for a regular income, which would mean working full-time always, which I continued to do without a break for the next twenty years. Now that A. had gone again, I was stretched to the limits of my capacity. I had to pay the rent and look after the furnished house; I had a full-time job, the children, the house and two paying guests to look after and cook for. I had to be up early to provide breakfast for everyone, clean the house, leave the children with the child-minder and get to work. On the way back I had to collect the children, then provide an evening meal for them and the paying guests. The rent of the furnished house was considerable and, even with the assistance of the paying guests, I could hardly make ends meet. The house had a garage up a back alley and I let this for 5/- a week to a man who at weekends serviced one or two cars. This just eased my situation sufficiently to make my finances balance. However, the neighbours complained about the mechanic. He had to go and I lost the 5/-.

I was heartbroken at the repetition of events. Anything is bearable once. The same thing twice or three times is unendurable. When something excruciatingly painful or sorrowful happens to us, we say to God: 'Do anything you like with me, I'll bear anything for you – only please not *that* again.' But often *that* is just what God does want and ask from us – because it is the only thing we would withhold. All my hopes and reconstituted trust lay in ruins. I tasted the depths of despair. In the lonely nights, exhausted with the stress of trying to keep going and remain solvent, I wept and wept. I wept for myself, for A., for the children, for the sadness of what ought not to be. I wept until there were no more tears left – for twenty-five years I never shed another tear. For the only time in my life, I never wanted to wake or see the light of a new day.

The interference of the neighbours was the breaking point. I was deeply hurt by the cruelty of their action, since they must have known about A. I felt crushed and unable to counteract their censure. I was beaten. I gave in, ceased to fight and retreated and, in so doing, for the only time abandoned A. I had an acquaintance in a somewhat similar position to me who had a daughter about the same age as G. She was house-keeping for an elderly man with a large house on Barnes Common. There was room for me and the children and the old man was willing to have us, but on no account A. when he was released. So I gave up the furnished house as quickly as I could and with the children went to live in the house at Barnes. This meant A. had nowhere to go when, before long, he came out of prison; he had to find digs for himself. This he did quite near and visited us often, but I think he never forgave me for that action which, to him, must have seemed a betrayal.

Before long we had found rooms in South Ealing, where we could all be together again. From then on, although there were one or two other incidents, the consequences were not so grave and there were no more major disasters of which I was aware. There were always events and actions which caused suspicions, but these were unresolved and with the passing of time I would be lulled back into a blessed sense of security. A. took a job as a porter in the West Middlesex Hospital, where he remained for several years. He still insisted upon the original story of his family background and that what was happening was due to the F.O. discrediting him. He constantly raised my hopes with his promises that sooner or later he would be reinstated, with a large sum of back pay, and that the house in the New Forest would be handed back. All this would be embellished with detail and seeming supporting facts. It was like manna in the desert to me.

However, I never said anything about it to anyone – in case it was not true. My respect for the truth did not allow me to make statements which might be lies. Yet my whole life was a lie. I was forced to act a lie, to the children and to everyone else. It would have been impossible and too

48

hurtful to have told the children the truth, and no part of it could be told without the whole. Rightly or wrongly, I always protected them from the disillusionment which I had had to suffer. I could not destroy the love and respect they had for their father and to admit their illegitimacy would have been far more traumatic for them than in today's conditions. I hated living a lie, but I was trapped into it and there was no escape. One of the attractions of A. was what appeared to be his exceptional modesty. If what he claimed was true, if he was indeed a Colonel in the Indian Army, then to be prepared to work as a hospital porter without making any fuss or bother about it, would indeed be meritorious. Actually, it was an inverted pride. I suspect that at work he gradually gave indications of who or what he purported to be so that his colleagues ended up admiring him for what he was doing.

Now that we were together again, I set to work once more slowly to rebuild the framework of hope and trust. It was a hard life, having to work full-time continually with no respite, other than two weeks' annual holiday, look after the house with no help and no aids of any kind, knit, make and mend for the children, and eke out the meagre resources to feed the family. I remember what a luxury it was when, having a few shillings to spare, I was able to take the sheets to the launderette. G. & N. were latch-key children, having to let themselves into an empty house on their return from school, but they did not seem to suffer any ill effects. I used to leave everything set out and prepared so that they could get themselves a meal and in the holidays I used to go back home in the lunch hour to get them a meal. The worst problems arose when they were ill, when I was torn between loyalty to them and to my work, sometimes having to leave them in bed surrounded by all that they needed, returning home once or twice during the day to see that they were all right.

49

In spite of everything, I was basically very happy. I loved and I had love – A. and the children, and I knew this was of more eternal value than any amount of possessions or material security. My brother was a successful radiologist, living in a high-class area in the comfort and security expected from our upbringing. He was married, but had no children. I never envied him. Somehow, deep within, I knew that my way, the way of suffering and a degree of deprivation, was the better way.

In addition to accepting the pinch of poverty, I had soon realised that I had to renounce any literary aspirations. The turmoil of my life made writing out of the question, nor did it leave me time for any of the meditative and philosophically orientated reading in which I had always taken such delight. I had to be content with getting through only an occasional and much lighter type of book. Self-fulfilment was sacrificed on the altar of love, and again it was not hard. Indeed, I was somewhat surprised, relieved and gratified to find when the children were very small, how naturally and easily parental love curbs and corrects our egoistic tendencies. Whilst we could indulge ourselves by drinking their tea ration, their meagre ration of the really luscious things – sweets, fruit etc. – had to be reinforced with ours. When I found that I could hand over my apples, to which I had always been addicted, without a pang, then I knew that mother love was in a healthy condition!

I learned that love makes every sacrifice in its favour, large or small, ultimately insignificant. It is its own reward. Nevertheless, the ceaseless grind of physical and mental stress took its toll upon me. I was always physically tired and often, when late in the evening, I finally achieved a chair, would sink into it too exhausted to move a muscle. Fear was always ready to spring to the surface. I must have answered every unexpected knock on the door like a frightened rabbit, apprehensive lest I was going to be confronted by police officers. I hated the sight of a Black Maria. I suppose I compensated for what I felt was my socially shameful situation with cleanliness; if we could not be rich, at least we could be clean. Consequently, everything had to be spick and span; I scrubbed and scoured and probably did more washing and ironing than was necessary. I did the housework according to a rota, certain things on certain days, and woe betide the child who made a dirty footprint on the doorstep I had just washed.

A. was very good with the children and in looking after them, and there were certain things he would do, such as clean and light the fire in the morning but, by today's standards, the help he gave me was very limited. What I resented was the ruthless round of continuity, the fact that there was never any let-up from the exhausting routine that although I, too, had a full-time job, only I was expected to perform all the domestic chores. Exhaustion, frustration and resentment expressed themselves in a truly vicious temper. The slightest thing that upset me or my schedule, or would add to it, something spilt on a clean cloth, something broken that would have to be replaced, would within seconds turn me into a veritable virago. I shouted and stormed at the least provocation. When I look back upon it, I think I must have been impossible to live with. My love drove me to provide the best home and background I could for the family, sacrificing myself in the process, but it would have been far better if I had relaxed and, to a certain extent, let things go, concentrating instead on creating loving relationships. This was left to A.

I was the unruly element in the home. I applied the heavy-handed discipline with the children. He was the peacemaker; he supplied the gentle, loving element, whilst nevertheless demanding a high standard from them and sometimes being severe. Although there were often rows between us, he endured my tantrums with great patience.

He was a 'good husband', I was a 'turbulent wife'. I look back with shame at my behaviour. The modern attitude, in which there is a much greater degree of untidiness and latitude in the home, but more emphasis on fostering loving relationships, is preferable, though not ideal. I should have been able to see and accept that the ideal was unattainable and ceased sacrificing peace and harmony on the altar of domesticity.

Nevertheless, apart from the jarring note I created, and in spite of our frequent moves, it was a happy and stable home background. I was extremely careful to protect the children from any crisis that might be taking place and never to convey to them the least shred of my suspicions regarding A. Love for them and for one another, which underpinned all our shortcomings and failures, provided the stability that was otherwise lacking. There came a time when we were able to go away for our first holiday – to Worthing – and after that there were several happy seaside holidays. A photograph album gives the impression of an ordinary, happy family; and so it was to all intents and purposes.

The boys grew up, did well at school and obtained free and assisted places at a minor public day school. For a number of years life proceeded smoothly, there were no more crises and we were able to pay our way without the gnawing anxiety of debt. In 1958 my mother died and the capital of which she was trustee and her furniture, which had been twenty years in store whilst she moved from place to place, was divided between my brother and myself. There was sufficient for us to obtain a mortgage on a house in Ealing, and so at last after seventeen rootless years we were able to have our own home and furniture. There we spent the last five years, and the happiest and most stable and 'respectable', of our life together.

G. entered Dartmouth, N. became head boy. A. was now getting on in years, being older than I realised. He had left the hospital and said he had returned to work at the F.O. He went to work regularly every day. There was supposed to be some connection with Sandersons, where, he said, his work sometimes took him. During this time he had three severe coronary attacks and was in hospital several weeks each time. Since the hospital was just round the corner, I was able to visit him every day. He suffered a great deal of pain and inconvenience from his condition and I lived in a constant state of anxiety. Whilst I did everything I could to make things easy for him, relieve him of any stress, give him the right diet, fear petrified me. We did not talk about death; it was an unmentionable spectre which turned tenderness into aloofness. I clothed myself in armour to oppose and keep at bay what I knew was approaching. Each time, after recovering, he went back to work, supposedly at the F.O. His statements and explanations became more exaggerated until, at the very end, they were so extravagant that they defied even my will to believe.

For years now I had been attending Mass with A. and the children. I longed to be able to kneel with them at the altar rails and receive Christ in the Blessed Sacrament. I used to gaze at the faces of the communicants returning to their places. They were distant and recollected, communing with an invisible presence. They had something, something not to be found in the Church of England; something that I coveted. If only we could all kneel together as a family and receive Our Lord, that, I felt, would be sign of his forgiveness. Everything would then be 'all right'.

In the early days A. had refrained from receiving Communion, although he had always continued to attend Mass, to take the children regularly and conscientiously to instruct them in the faith. At the time of G.'s first Communion he returned to the Sacrament, saying he had been to Confession. If, as he so persistently maintained, his first marriage had been annulled before our ceremony, then we

53

were validly married and there was, of course, no reason why he should not receive the sacraments. My conscience, however, could not rest there. I could not ask for reception into the Church without revealing to the priest concerned the whole situation as I understood it and I knew that, as indeed was the case, he would require documentary evidence of the annulment. This A. could not provide, maintaining that the documents had been destroyed in the bombing. I could not understand and felt a great sadness and some resentment towards God that I, who had married in good faith and contrition for my prior sin, was debarred from his gift of himself, whilst A., who had been guilty of at least deception, was allowed to receive him. I ached with exclusion from something for which I longed. Christ's words: 'He who eats my flesh and drinks my blood has eternal life, and I will raise him up at the last day' had imprinted themselves on my mind with magnetic force; I did not want to be excluded from eternal life. The door was the Eucharist; when I knelt at the altar rail I would be a member of the community, my sins would have been forgiven. The reception of Our Lord's gift of himself in the Sacrament would be the fulfilment of my return, the ratification of forgiveness.

I was knocking at the door, but it was barred and there was no way in. I could not be received into the Church unless either I could show I was validly married to A. or I left him. For years I was locked in this predicament, to which there seemed no solution. If I was asked why I dallied so long on the threshold, I used to say that it was because I was not yet sure. I was sure, but I did not know how to open the door. Several years before, one of the staff in the firm where I worked, who had converted and knew I was interested in the Catholic Church, persuaded me to go and talk with a Jesuit at Farm Street, thinking no doubt that he would be able to resolve whatever was keeping me from taking the final plunge. I made an appointment and went along to see him. It required all my courage, because I was going to have to tell him the whole sordid story of the 'marriage', which I had never yet revealed. This, at least, my mother and brother never knew; I had never told anyone or discussed it with anyone. I was shown into a room, and there I waited in my misery and anxiety for about an hour and a half. Eventually a very contrite Jesuit arrived, admitting that he had been out to lunch and had forgotten the appointment. Feeling even more shamed at the contrast between the pleasant social engagement he had just enjoyed and the sordid disclosure I was about to make, I told him the whole story. He could offer no help and no solution. He merely said that I must wait, by which I knew that he meant until I was released by A.'s death.

The door may have been locked, but God did not cease to call and draw me towards the Church. At the end of 1962 I could resist the inward goading no longer, but I did not know to whom, to which priest to go for help. I knew, because of the nature of the situation, I had to be careful in my selection. One day, after praying fervently in Ealing Abbey for guidance on the matter, as I came down the steps a monk I knew spoke to me, chatted a bit and then said: 'If there is ever anything I can do for you, let me know.' Then he repeated his statement more emphatically. I knew this was God's answer to my prayer and that he was the one to whom I must go. I told him the whole story and, as I had suspected, he insisted the annulment would have to be confirmed, undertaking to discuss it with A. and then put the wheels in motion in Rome for official ratification. Meanwhile, I was to start instruction. He did, however, warn me that, as I well knew, A. was gravely ill and that the stress of the investigations might hasten his death. The pull God was exerting, though hidden, was now irresistible, overcoming my natural fears and anxieties. I told him to proceed. The matter had to be brought to a conclusion; if

A.'s assertions were shown to be false then, I felt, he would be forced to retract and be properly reconciled with God and the Church through the sacrament of Confession. Even if this were to kill him, it would be preferable to his continuing to live a lie and, possibly, die in sacrilege. If, on the contrary, he was vindicated, there would be no problem.

Although a complete tiro, I had always been keenly interested in and stimulated by any form of doctrinal reasoning or argument and had begun to dabble in St. Thomas's *Summa*. I therefore relished the instructions. In January 1963 they had to be postponed whilst I went into hospital for a hysterectomy. I had been having so much pain that sometimes I had had to crawl up the stairs on my hands and knees to reach my bed and lie down. Again, following the operation I developed a severe infection, my temperature shot up, I was semi-delirious and could not recognise the office colleagues when they visited me. For several days I was wracked with pain and in acute discomfort from accompanying complications. Very acute pain narrows existence down to a pinpoint. Everything else drops away and has no relevance. For three or four days there was nothing but the pain and the drug, which for a little while only gave some relief. My eyes were glued to the clock watching the second hand as it ticked off the seconds and minutes until the blessed moment arrived when the next dose was due. At the end of a week, when I began to get better and the pain eased, I realised that I had been too carried away by the intensity of the pain to think of offering it up to God. It seemed a pity to have missed such an opportunity when there was so much for which I had to do penance and make restitution. However, I did not feel it mattered because my disposition had been one of acceptance.

Whilst I had always been attracted by the liturgy, Anglican in my earlier days and Catholic later, and had relished any doctrinal crumbs that came my way, I had never developed my prayer life. I prayed only a minimum amount, a few hurried prayers last thing at night, often omitted, possibly for long periods, until the pricking of conscience or some new crisis would goad me into starting again. Under the impetus of the instructions, the knowledge that A. was gravely ill, and the constant dread of his suffering a further and fatal attack, I made a real effort to be faithful to some very basic morning and evening prayers. Ten minutes' prayer at night seemed an eternity, during which I would fidget and long for the time when I could get into bed. I tried to say the Our Father with attention and meaning, but I knew I was withholding consent to 'thy will be done': I could not bond my will for the extension of A.'s life to conform to the Almighty's will to separate us. I felt that to surrender would be to betray A. into the hands of death, to betray our love. I tried gallantly, but I never succeeded – I could not let A. go, I could not hand him over to God. But I had tried, and that was all God asked of me that he might crown my puny effort. Like the blurred outline of a familiar object glimpsed through a break in swirling mists, gently, indefinably, so softly as to be only just recognisable, he penetrated my background consciousness, emerging as what I can only describe as 'a friend'. God was my friend. With that knowledge I began to experience a peace of conscience which I had never previously known.

About this time something rather strange occurred. My brother was an unenthusiastic Anglican, like so many attending morning service when he felt like it. However, he had extremely high principles and could not easily tolerate any deviance. Knowing a good deal, suspecting more no doubt, he would have nothing to do with A. and never invited him to their house. I would go alone to spend a day there. Sometimes the children would be invited to stay in their school holidays. We always maintained a cordial relationship, but we never discussed A. I knew my brother was highly critical and suspicious and, if it had come to an argument, would have demolished me for the simple reason that I had only belief and no facts with which to defend A. Moreover, I did not want to be placed in a situation in which, in formulating my hopes, I could be uttering lies. I preferred to say nothing and was careful to keep it like that.

My brother respected my feelings. He was deeply grieved at the way my life had developed and would encourage anything, provided he considered it morally acceptable, which would bring me happiness or ease my situation. He was, therefore, quite supportive of my being received into the Church. He told me he wanted me to meet the couple who lived in the next house, because he felt we would have a lot in common; she was a convert and had been at Wycombe Abbey. Directly I saw her, I knew I wanted her to be my sponsor at my Confirmation after I had been received. This, in due course, she was, and it was through an introduction contrived by her that my subsequent life took the course it did. There is no doubt whatever that God worked through her.

She was very concerned about people, seeking to manage or influence them for their own good. She was the mother of a large, grown-up family, kind and hospitable, but themselves living very frugally. She gave the impression of being torn between her conservative upbringing and the progressive and socialistic ideas of her barrister husband. But the strange thing was that she lent me a book called *Those Whom God Has Not Joined*, which was a factual book about a couple caught in a somewhat similar situation as A. and myself, unable to marry. Eventually they realised that the only solution to their predicament was to remain together, but living as brother and sister. Only thus could they live in freedom of conscience, reconciled to and in full communion with the Church, whilst yet retaining their love and the companionship which was so vital to their well-being. There is no way

58

in which my new friend could have known my situation. Even if my brother had known, which I am sure he did not, he would never have told her: he would have been only too anxious to keep it quiet.

When I read that book it seemed to speak directly to me and to be indicating the path A. and I had to adopt. Deeply impressed, I gave it to A. to read. He promised to do so and said he had taken it to work. When he died I found it in his drawer. Whether he ever read it, I do not know. However, we agreed to adopt the same measure, and that was how it was for the few weeks left until he died. On account of my post-operative condition and A.'s cardiac condition, it was never really put to the test. However, the intention was firmly established, on my part at least. So strange were the circumstances in which the book came into my hands that I could not see it otherwise than as an invitation from God to an act of obedience in atonement for our original act of disobedience.

Chapter 5

It took me a long time to recover from the operation. I had been too exhausted and stressed when I had it. I was so weak that for two or three weeks after my return home any small household chore such as ironing or pushing the sweeper over the floor would make me pant and gasp for breath. After three months the surgeon allowed me to go back to work part-time.

On the evening of my second day back, 4th April, A. dropped dead. He had obviously been very ill when I went into hospital, and the anxiety of having to leave him to cope alone with the children had exacerbated my condition. However, he had recovered sufficiently to return to work and had been to work the day he died. After my part-time day, I had gone to an instruction in the early evening. On returning home, as I opened the front door, I had a sensation which I can only describe as the Angel of Death going out as I came in. I knew instantaneously, before I set foot in the house, that something was very wrong. The house was wrapped in silence, a thick, deathly hush. I looked in the sitting-room; it was empty. I moved quickly to the kitchen, and there I found him on the floor. He must have died instantaneously, falling backwards and hitting his head with great force on the floor. He had not been dead long. I sent for the priest who, I think, anointed him. That I had known this could happen at any moment made no difference. I was stunned, stupefied and desolate at losing him. He had told me that there was a secret compartment in his wallet containing papers verifying his identity, which I would find after he died. I suggested to the priest that perhaps we ought to remove his wallet before the undertakers came. I have often wondered what he thought; no doubt he was shocked, thinking I could not wait to get my hands on the money. But how wrong we can be in our judgments. I did not want the money; I wanted the verification for which I so yearned. There was no special compartment, and no verification.

Once A. was dead the blows fell thick and fast. God tore the bandages from my eyes, forcing upon me the revelation which I had so persistently resisted. All that had gone before was as nothing compared to what happened now. I was passive. I did not have to do anything. Things just happened over which I had no control. Obstacles took on gigantic proportions, disillusionment was total.

At first no doctor would come to assure me that he actually was dead; it took days and much trouble to obtain a death certificate, the doctors who had attended him being away. That night I found photographs and sufficient evidence to throw sickening light on previous incidents, making it clear that he had not been faithful. Then I found notes for a novel, in which I could not fail to recognise a portrait of myself – myself at my ugliest and most shameful worst. This would not have mattered, to my sorrow it was only too true – but it was written with malice. There were also notes attributing malicious intentions to certain actions of mine which were entirely innocent. Only malice sees malice where there is none. This was the death blow to my belief that he had loved me. All the other things he could have done out of weakness, still loving me, but not this. Love *could* not write such things, could not even think them. Love excuses, protects; love hides the defects of the beloved, even from herself. There was no love there, only a warped mind. Perhaps that is the answer to the riddle of his character, since only three months earlier he had been writing very loving letters to me whilst I was in hospital and he had been too ill with his heart condition to visit me in the icy winter weather.

Letters of condolence came from colleagues at work – Sandersons. It was then clear that that was where he was working right up to the end and had been for a considerable time. I knew nothing at all about the writers, the circumstances they mentioned, the place, the conditions, type of work he had been doing or anything else; I had to reply being careful not to betray my ignorance. It was clear that this was the reality and that the assertions about the F.O., the names of the personnel, the little details thrown in from time to time, were all pure fiction. He had gone out every day, but to somewhere and to a life of which I knew nothing.

Because I wanted to prevent the boys from finding out any of the facts about A., I had to keep all the arrangements strictly under my control and not seek their help as I would otherwise have done. Now that his statement about his work, at any rate since he had claimed to have returned to the F.O., had been shown to be pure fabrication, it was probable all the rest was equally unfounded and I was fearful of what was going to be uncovered. First I had to inform his wife of his death. I have no recollection how I did so, but the two sons came up to see me. They were quite pleasant, but insisted that he be buried under his proper Christian names and the correct date of birth, which meant that he was in his seventieth year, and that he be buried not in Ealing as I had arranged, but in Portsmouth, where there was a grave reserved with a place for their mother.

When they had gone, I had to go to the undertaker to make the necessary alterations. I remember walking up and down outside the premises, panic stricken. The names I had given and which were already on the coffin and the death certificate were those he had claimed from the Marlborough connection and the date of birth was seven years later. I thought that by requesting the alterations I would be unleashing a hive of police enquiries. Would they not ask why I did not know who I was burying? And surely it must be illegal to bury someone with a different identity from that on the death certificate? I walked up and down the street, distraught, unable to go in, then in desperation phoned the priest who was instructing me; he put me on to a solicitor. Strangely, it did not seem to matter. I could have the nameplate changed without any problem. So I went back to the office of the undertakers who received my instructions for the new plate and burial at Portsmouth without any disturbance to his habitual suavity. To me it seemed an enormity; to him it was all in the day's work. No doubt it is quite common for people to do the strangest things under the stress of grief.

Total and definitive disillusionment came when the two sons assured me that there had never been any divorce nor any annulment. This was the lynchpin, to me the most vital issue and that to which A. had most persistently clung. Now, at last, I had to accept that not only was it all a pack of lies but, worse, he had died in sacrilege. With the situation as it was, there is no way in which he could legitimately have received the sacraments. Yet he was receiving Communion regularly up to his death. One cannot even hope for a last-minute confession, because he continued to deceive the priest who was searching for corroboration of the annulment. He never retracted this, as he would have had to have done had he reformed. It was left to me to tell the priest that there were no papers to be found. So appalling did this seem to me that I asked our parish priest not to preach any homily at the Requiem. I was afraid he would extol A.'s apparent virtues which, in the circumstances, would have been unendurable, adding sacrilege to sacrilege, in which I could bear to have no part and which I would have wanted to denounce. Consequently, when asked if I wished A.'s body to rest overnight in front of the Blessed Sacrament, I said, 'No.' It would have been yet further sacrilege. I was acutely conscious of the holiness and majesty of God; he was a God of Truth, to be feared, reverenced and obeyed. I had not yet encountered the tenderness and mercy of the God who is Love.

For the first time, I felt the consoling strength of the Church. I received many letters from the Catholic community of school and parents, all assuring me of prayers and many having Masses said for A. Although not yet received, I felt truly part of the Body that is the Church, an ailing limb towards which the rest of the Body was acting with concern and compassion: I felt united with them in belief and purpose.

The church was surprisingly full for A.'s requiem and I was touched to see several of the boys from N.'s school. The Mass, with no homily, was soon over. To add to the macabre situation, the body had to be whisked hurriedly away for a post-mortem before being taken down to Portsmouth the following day for burial. That journey to Portsmouth, following the coffin, was a torment: grief and anxiety overwhelmed me. I had no idea what was going to happen or what course events would take. At the graveside we would meet A.'s wife, his daughter and the two sons. I had had to adopt A.'s deception and tell G. & N. that they were his sister-in-law, nephews and niece. I did not know whether they would say anything which would expose the truth. I did not know what the procedure was at a Catholic funeral, let alone this one. I wondered what the undertakers thought was going on, and how much, if anything, they knew. What would 'she' be like? Who would take precedence at the graveside? All the way I was petrified with anxiety to protect G. & N. from the awful truth. I could not bear, least of all at this moment, to shatter their love and respect for their father.

We met at the graveside; an elderly, sad, nondescript-looking woman. We all huddled round the grave. It was a very simple ceremony and no problems arose. I suppose the two groups spoke to each other, but nothing significant was said and we separated, G. & N. still unaware of anything untoward. That, at least, was a relief, and the journey back was that much better. I had made arrangements with the undertakers for a tombstone to be engraved and erected but, when I informed the other family, they flatly refused to allow it, saying that they would arrange the matter. There was nothing I could do; I had no legal status or rights. When I visited the grave some years later, nothing had been done. So he who in life lied his true identity out of existence, is equally nameless in death; he lies in an unnamed grave, an unresolved enigma.

One more blow had yet to fall. A month or two after A.'s death I found documents showing he had been receiving a grant from the Education Authorities for the boys, so naturally I applied for its renewal. I, of course, gave correct details of my income which, apparently, were inconsistent with what had gone before. There was an enquiry and I was threatened with a charge for obtaining money under false pretences. I was called before a panel where documents, ranging over several years, were put before me giving false facts about our income. I had never seen those documents, let alone signed them, yet they contained perfect facsimiles of my signature. Fortunately, the authorities believed my denial of any implication, but I had to pay back £300 (which I had never seen) and which was a lot of money then and a severe strain on my meagre resources, but it was offered lovingly and gratefully to God as reparation for the enormity of the crime. It was radical betrayal. A. knew that never, under any circumstances, would I sign any papers giving a false declaration. All along he had betrayed his own integrity, but now in my name he had deliberately betrayed the principles which he knew I held to be inviolable: he had *used* me to obtain his own dishonest ends.

At last the flame of hope, which I had so long and so lovingly fostered, was snuffed. Totally disillusioned, I now saw with dreadful clarity the truth which I had lacked the courage to face. God had taken matters into his own hands; he had rained blows upon me, stripping me one by one of my illusions, until there was *nothing* left. What God does, he does perfectly. Never was anyone so annihilated. I realised there was not a single thing A. had ever told me that I could put my finger on and now say 'that is true'. I knew nothing of his childhood, parents, family, background, schooling, his supposed time in India, in the Army, in the war, what had actually occurred as regards the F.O., of not only the years before he met me but of the twenty-two years of our life together, and finally of the circumstances of his work at Sandersons. Just one thing I knew – he had written intelligence stories. I had seen correspondence with the publishers, had handled the books, had even watched him write a new one which was never published – but they were fiction and told me nothing of the true situation. This indeed was the supreme irony: the only reality in a mountain of fiction was fiction itself.

For the rest, the only things of which I had proof were his lies, and I had discovered enough to realise it was but the tip of the iceberg. There was no memory of him that I could retain and know that it was true. Every conversation we had had, important and unimportant, had been a lie; if I asked him to supply facts about himself so that I could become a Catholic, his answer was a lie: if I asked him what he had done that day, it was still a lie. He was one vast lie.

He had not only died, he had evaporated into nothing. There was no one left, because where there is no truth there is no person. He had destroyed himself; there was nothing left but a heap of ashes; my love was reduced to a heap of ashes.

My grief was overwhelming, but throughout I never shed a tear. It was beyond tears; it was too awful to be assuaged by the consolation which tears can bring. In any case, there were none left; I had shed them all fifteen years before. I still loved him, and I grieved at his loss. He was all I had ever wanted, and to be with him was fulfilment enough, whatever the accompanying circumstances. But far, far worse was my grief at the wrongness of it. I was forced to accept that he had died unrepentant and, worse, in sacrilege, and that thereby, according to the teaching of the Church, had cut himself off from eternal life.

He died on 4th April, the Thursday before Holy Week. There was, therefore, only just time for his requiem and burial the following Tuesday and Wednesday before the commencement of the Easter liturgy. For me it was, indeed, a living out, a participation in the Passion. I attended all the Holy Week and Easter ceremonies. The sad, solemn liturgy preceding the Day of Resurrection took me into a new dimension in which the enormity of sin was manifested in all its horrifying reality. I knew then that sin is the only true tragedy. What we call tragedies are not so in the real sense, because ultimately all is redeemable. However sad, however much the relatives grieve, ultimately the death of a child or a person in the prime of life is not a tragedy. Their virtue survives them as they cross over into eternal life. But the death of one who by his obstinacy makes himself unredeemable, is death indeed.

It was the lost potential which broke my heart. The contrast between what he could have been and what he was. He could have been what he was in the home, the virtuous, dearly loved and very loveable partner and parent. But that aspect of him was not true in the light of his other, deviant, side, by which it was vitiated. There must be integrity of person, you cannot be two different people; a house divided against itself falls. So persistent, all-embracing and deep-seated was the deceit he had practised that he had destroyed himself. Sin is defined as a lack of the good which should be. Deceit is a deprivation of truth. I sometimes felt that that deprivation had gone so far that he had annihilated the truth of his being and that he had indeed ceased to exist, but my faith told me that, once created, God never ceases to hold the soul of man in existence. It was the lost goodness, beyond hope of recovery, which was the unbearable anguish. It was a descent into hell; as hope died, I died of the pain of it. It was as if goodness itself had died – A.'s goodness, my goodness, everyone's goodness.

I did not allow myself to become resentful. I had loved him and I wanted to go on loving him – even though there was nothing left to love. I knew that if once resentful thoughts were allowed to take hold, love would die. Looking back afterwards, it seemed as if an angel had sat on a chest full of resentful thoughts in my mind, keeping the lid down. I did, however, feel some resentment that he had, as it were, slipped away and I was left to carry the load of sin and pay the penalty of it all – not only mine, but his as well. I could not help feeling that his sinfulness was worse than mine. I had voluntarily walked into the sin that sprung the trap, but he had set the trap. However, in its weight blame could not be apportioned: it was one inextricably mingled burden of sin. The cross that was laid upon my back was consciousness of sin, and the more my consciousness sharpened, the heavier the load became.

That Easter and for the following three months, I carried a crushing burden, in the form of a mound of sin. Its weight was sadness, a sadness that seeped into every part of my being. There was no one with whom to share my grief, neither the boys nor anyone else knew anything of its origin, and indeed I did not want to and could not share it. Who could understand the depth or bear the burden of my broken heart and desecrated love? All I wanted was, like a sick animal, to crawl away alone and lick my wounds. I was stunned, turned to stone with grief and sadness. So sad was I that I believed I would never smile again. I must indeed have been a depressing companion for the boys at home and the staff at work. I remember, having returned to the office after A.'s death, one day gazing down from the top-floor window into the court-yard below and being engulfed, deluged, in a great tide of sorrow, pain for what could have been, what should have been but was not. It must have been written on my face, because someone came up to me and said, 'Don't look so sad.' I then realised I was inflicting it on others and that I had to try to make an effort to act normally. But nothing cured the inner pain. It remained like lead in my heart.

It is because of the *accumulation* of suffering and the passive endurance of evils inflicted by others that the dying of Jesus is referred to as the Passion. We too, when sufferings escalate to an extraordinary level and evil is inflicted upon us, are invited to endure a little passion. From the moment of A.'s death, all initiative was taken out of my hands. My role was entirely passive. Revelation was forced upon me, grief was laid upon me. All I had to do and all I could do was to endure it. There was no way of escaping it and, like acute physical pain, it narrowed everything to a single point. Nothing else existed except the pain. Intense physical pain is not confined to the seat of origin, it radiates until the whole body becomes pain. We are pain, it possesses us, it dominates us, we cannot escape from it, we become pain itself. All life outside our pain ceases to exist, it is pinpointed down to the enduring of that pain and the hope of alleviation. Only afterwards are we fully aware of what we have suffered and that, in some obscure way, it has done something to us: we are both scarred and moulded. So it is with the anguish of heart. It possesses us entirely and nothing exists outside it. It presses down upon us with a terrible weight and crushes us. But for this pain there is no doctor, no drug and no remedy. It stretches into eternity; there is no hope of alleviation – facts cannot be altered. I went to work and did my job, but for the rest I just wanted to stay at home and be quiet. If you keep very still it may hurt less. That was how I was, still, quiet, dumb with grief. There was no light in the tunnel and I thought there never would be, because nothing, no power on earth, could alter what had happened. It was sealed with the finality of death.

Everyone has their measure of suffering allotted to them: I knew that, for me, A.'s death and all that went with it was the completion of the measure. In a way it was a relief – there could never be anything like it or anything worse, however long I lived. We die in accordance with the degree of inordinance in the love we have given to something or someone other than God. I had been wholly given to A., and all of me died. I was nothing but that pain, till the numbness of death slid over it.

Chapter 6

After A.'s death I continued with my instructions. I told the priest just sufficient for him to grasp the reality of the situation and to leave him in no doubt that there never had been any annulment. I still could not bring myself to reveal more than was necessary. He asked me if, in the light of what had happened, I wanted to continue instruction. I told him it made no difference. God and his Church were still the same; neither could be blamed for A.'s infidelity.

I enjoyed the instructions with their intellectual stimulus, soaking up the doctrine, much of which was new to me, like a dry sponge. It all fitted together and made sense, and in those areas where mystery prevailed and reason could not penetrate, faith gave firm and willing assent.

By the end of the instructions two points had firmly established themselves in my mind. One was that there is only one prayer: 'thy will be done'. The other was a doctrinal problem; I could not understand the continual 'coming and going' of Our Lord in the Eucharist. Whatever the practice, it seemed to me that theoretically it should only be necessary to receive Our Lord once – Maranatha – afterwards it would be a matter of he *has* come. I was in a completely unformed, subconscious way extraordinarily and acutely aware of the stupendous fact of God's coming and entering into us. I could not get it out of my mind that if God *really* came like that, if the all-omnipotent God entered in giving himself to be united to a person by being consumed into their body, and that person received him with pure intent to the best of their ability, then no evil could ever touch that person again. The goodness of God was so powerful that such an intimate contact with that Absolute Good *must* override and overcome all evil. God's coming would disperse all evil, and I could not understand how once being dispersed and goodness established, it could ever return. It seemed to me that that goodness must be its own protection. What God had made good by the touch of his presence, must be forever protected under the omnipotence of his goodness. Therefore I could not understand why it was really necessary to keep receiving Communion. I was thinking entirely in terms of the divinity of God without reference to the humanity of Our Lord Jesus Christ. It was a purely academic problem with no particular relevance to myself, except for the awareness of the tremendous significance of the fact of God's coming to man in this way. I was thinking solely in terms of objective goodness, not in those of grace, of sanctification, about which I knew nothing. It just seemed to me that was how it ought to be and I could not understand why it wasn't. I did not yet understand the workings of grace, the degree of God's condescension in coming to us, how he stoops and mutes his divinity.

Three months after A.'s death, the priest suddenly announced that no more instructions were necessary and that I was ready to be received into the Church.

My reception took place in the Lady Chapel of Ealing Abbey on 13th July 1963, only G. and N. being present. It was an ordeal, as I had to read a long profession of faith and I still had inhibitions about reading aloud. The abjuration of my Church of England faith, which was then still required, went against the grain, for it had given me a firm Christian foundation and sustained me in my youth.

Although my reception was the realisation of a long-sought and longed-for goal, there was no joy for me in the ceremony. I was still crushed by sadness. Directly I had become a member of the Roman Catholic Church, I was able to make my Confession, which took place immediately. Confession is never easy, but for a mid-life convert there is no dearth of material for the first. The anxiety is lest one omit anything important. G. & N., having carefully instructed me in the rite, were slightly disconcerted when, on my reappearance, I admitted having omitted to say the Act of Contrition at the proper time. But I knew it did not matter. I had been too transfixed by the beautiful and blessed words of absolution to be able to interrupt them with the Act of Contrition, as was the requirement. I never had a flicker of doubt that everything about that Confession was valid; I was not, as might be expected, overwhelmed by a great sense of relief now that all the sins of my past life, of which I had been so conscious, were forgiven – there was only a deepening of the peace of conscience which had been born when God became my friend.

I was to make my first Communion the following day, which was Sunday, at the eight o'clock Mass in our parish church, St. Peter & St. Paul's, Northfields. I prepared as best I could, getting up early and reading very carefully the preparatory prayers for Mass in the old Missal. The Tridentine Mass and the three hours' fast were still in force. Then, true to form, and transcending even my grief and the solemnity of the occasion, my femininity rose to the surface. What was I going to wear – on my head, that is? Of course it would have to be black, but was it to be a hat or a mantilla? On and off they went, until I finally opted for the latter as being more appropriate. God must have smiled.

Now the moment was coming when we would kneel together at the altar. I had longed for it, feeling that

75

receiving God together in this manner would be a pledge of his acceptance of us as a family. This was the real sign of reconciliation. But now that it was happening the family was mutilated; one was missing and the joy it should have been was turned to ashes. There was no easing of my grief; it was, if possible, even more intense. My heart was still like lead with the weight of sin and I was afraid lest, when I knelt with G. & N. each side of me, the poignancy of the situation would overwhelm me, releasing the tears which had never been shed. The boys ushered me into a pew, near the front on the left-hand side under the pulpit, the priest entered and the Mass began. The first shock came when the priest announced from the pulpit that the Mass was being said for my intention. Almost immediately a strange thought entered my head: this is the one true fairy story. Whatever I ask for now will come true. With such an opportunity, what was my intention to be? I had to think quickly, so that I could formulate it in my mind. It did not take long. I had only one wish, one concern, one prayer: for the forgiveness and salvation of A. However, I was not able to be entirely altruistic so, along with that, my major, all-embracing intention, I pushed in a little, very secondary one for myself: that I would always progress in the spiritual life. I knew that if one stops advancing, one slides back and I was afraid lest, having got where I was, I got no further.

As I stepped into the queue forming in the aisle to go up for Communion, I had a feeling I had never before experienced: something I could only describe as a sensation of perfect health, of total well-being. We moved up, the boys manipulated themselves so that I was between them. I knelt down, G. on one side, N. on the other . . .

I had gone into church dumb with grief; I came out still dumb – dumb with joy. As we left the priest was on the steps talking with parishioners. I was glad he did not speak to me. I was afraid that if he looked at me he would see God blazing out of my face.

What had happened in the fifteen minutes or so since I had knelt down? – That is the story of 'After'.

AFTER

Foreword

On that Sunday of my first Communion, I left the church as
stunned with joy as I had entered it stunned with grief.
Entering St. Peter & St. Paul's, Northfields, less than an hour
previously, although now at last a Catholic and about to
achieve my objective of receiving the gift of the true Bread
of Life, my sorrow still lay like lead upon my heart.

I walked out dumb with joy; God had made himself
known in the Eucharist. Just as the grief had been too big for
words or tears, so was the joy so intense and so profound
that it was beyond any form of outward expression. The
same reticence which had cloaked the indecency of my grief
now hid the unseemly exuberance of my joy.

What follows has, therefore, remained sealed in my heart
for twenty-three years, too sacred to be revealed to anyone
other than my spiritual director. I began relating it to him
when I met him a year after the event and continued the
account for several years in long letters. The disclosure I
made to him at our first meeting was the most precious gift
I have ever laid before another person. It was like giving
God to him. Although for years he had been steeped in God
and it was his function as a priest to mediate God through
the preaching of his word and the celebration of the sacraments, it was giving him God in a different perspective. It is
precious not for what it says of myself, but for what it tells
us about God, the God of our Fathers, of Abraham, Isaac, of

Our Lord Jesus Christ, Our Lady and all the saints, a God of steadfast love and faithfulness. It tells us nothing we did not know before from scripture and the Church's teaching. As my life begins to draw to its close, I realise I cannot die with so precious a gift locked in my heart. It is time to give God back to God, that is to compile an account which will be available to anyone whom he may elect to read it. What happens to it, whether it remains unread or whether many read it, is entirely in God's hands.

It is written at a time when the doctrine of the Real Presence is not fully understood or appreciated by many, when it is sometimes obscured or by default denied. I have never for a minute doubted that what happened on that first Sunday was a revelation of the Eucharist. In itself it was not something special – it was something that happens every time the Eucharist is celebrated to all those who fully participate in it. It was a revelation of what happens, how grace is bestowed, in the Eucharist. *It was the Eucharist.* It was theology in the real sense (the word *about God*), conceptualised knowing, emerging into another dimension, experiential knowing. It was theology confirmed in the lived experience of that which it affirms about God. There is no conflict between the intellectual and the experiential; the doctrine which the Church teaches and what is experienced are a perfect unity, two sides of a single coin.

This account is written in homage and witness. It is written in everlasting adoration and gratitude for the mercy and goodness of God, the extent of which can be more profoundly known by experience than by intellect, but which still infinitely exceeds even our graced powers of apprehension. It is written in witness, in witness to the reality of the Real Presence. Just as the apostles had witness to the resurrection, of which they had experiential evidence, so am I constrained to write this witness to the Real Presence of our Lord and Saviour Jesus Christ in the blessed sacrament of the Eucharist.

Chapter 1

I felt Him come; I felt Him approach from the right along the line of kneeling communicants. He came with the priest, slowly approaching, drawing nearer, a radiance with no light. First, I was aware of a strong fragrance, like that of incense. I thought: it is the scent of incense clinging to the priest's vestments. It increased as the priest approached, and with it came a warmth – like none on earth. It wrapped me round and touched my flesh; lighter than a feather, sweeter than any known sensation, it grew in intensity as He approached. It was a human touch, deified, conveying to the senses gentleness and tenderness of infinite, divine origin, enrapturing them as they surrendered to the sweetness which held them in thrall. It was the touch of the Divine Lover, the God-Man Jesus. I was wrapped and enfolded in Love.

The priest drew level with me, holding the ciborium very low, below the level of my chin and, as he selected a Host to give to me, I looked down into the ciborium. As I did so, I heard a voice which seemed to come straight through my back between my shoulder-blades, say: 'So *this* is God.' Each word was clearly and precisely enunciated. The sweetness of his nearness was now overpowering. I lifted my chin and put out my tongue as I had been instructed but, before my eyelids came down, I felt my eyeballs rolling upwards as if I was going into trance. The priest placed the

Sacred Host on my tongue. It was spherical, not flat, yet there was nothing there – *it had no substance*. Lighter than the Love that had caressed my flesh, it disintegrated on the instant of contact. There was nothing there – only Him. But now He was within.

The same warm, tender ray of love was spreading within me, expanding all the time, growing in intensity as it permeated through my body to every cell of my being. It was a radiance of unearthly warmth, a spiritual presence, with no shape or material form, with the quality of subtlety; but it was felt not just as a power or a presence, but as a *Person* wholly occupied in revealing his love and bestowing the gift of himself in an intimate, unique and singular relationship. It was Jesus who is God, veiling his divinity in unutterable tenderness. Tenderness in a man is a lovely thing, the muting of strength in the face of weakness. In God it ravishes the soul it caresses, so great is the contrast of divine omnipotence expressed in such exceeding gentleness, so infinite the consideration and respect for the human soul He enters. But now He took on as well the attribute of glory; I was filled with the risen, glorified Christ. His glory is felt and recognised as a previously unknown element, because there is no human counterpart. It is a vitality and power radiating into the whole person, yet muted in unfathomable tenderness. He conveys unmistakably that He is the glorified, risen Christ; He allows his glory to be felt but, lest it sear, He wraps it in ineffable gentleness.

Whilst the senses were invaded and taken over by this power entirely beyond their control, yet so inconceivably gentle and tender, the mind stood back and observed. Every nerve of my whole person, body, soul, will, intellect, was locked in concentration upon what was taking place. Yet I was able to think: I shall not be able to get up from the altar rails. I shall be rooted to the spot. But I did get up and move back to my pew.

It was still the same – He was still there within me. And then, as I knelt in my pew, something very strange happened. My heart whispered: 'Sweet, sweet Jesus.' The words came straight from my heart, but they were not my words. They were as alien to me as if they had been in a foreign language. I would never have used such a combination which, for me, would have had an abhorrently sentimental connotation. They came from an impenetrable depth, somewhere far beyond time, eternity itself. They were not loud and clear words, as had been 'So this is God', to be heard with the inner ear, nor had they any origin in my mind. They were the softest of whispers. The heart is dumb, it knows only how to love and suffer; but that day it was endowed with speech in order that it might whisper to the other heart within. As surely as the other words had come from without, these words came from within, literally from the depths of my heart – but they were not my words. They were given, affirming Jesus, whom I had already recognised in the first touch of his caress. In them I knew the true meaning of the word 'sweet' and that this was the perfect adjective to describe Jesus. He came not only as Lord and Christ, but as Jesus, the Divine Healer, whose name contains beatitude in its mere utterance. And from the heart that had whispered 'Sweet, sweet Jesus', I now whispered my request: 'Jesus, forgive him.' This most simple exchange is the impenetrable core of the mystery of his coming. Later, after it was all over, I was filled with deep gratitude and relief that I had been able to make this act of petition whilst the union was at its height. Such was the power of the occasion that it was a once-for-all act: a definitive handing over. A. no longer was my responsibility; he had gone from me into the mercy of that unfathomable love.

I don't know how long Jesus stayed with me as I knelt there in my pew; it must have been some minutes, and all the time his inward presence, penetrating, saturating my whole being with his muted glory, increased in intensity. Suddenly, instantaneously, without any warning, He was gone; totally vanished, as if He had never been. He came gently, increasingly, stealing softly upon me; his leaving was the most instantaneous thing I have ever experienced – quicker than time. One split second I was full of Him, full of the fullness of the Deity, the next He was gone, without leaving a vestige of himself or his going. There was nothing left but me, and without Him there was no longer any me. There was nothing but emptiness, an emptiness which was the total contrast of the fullness of a second before. The desperation, the pain, the sorrow, the anguish of having lost what had been there is indescribable. Had that emptiness lasted, there is no way in which I could have continued to live. I knew then that I could not live without what I had been given and had lost. Without it there was no life, there was nothing – *absolutely nothing*: life could not be lived. I would have gone home and lain down and died. Nothing in heaven or earth could recompense or console me for that which I had had and which had been taken away. I sank into the despair of an intolerable grief – there was no way I could make Him come back; He had come and He had gone.

I don't know how long it lasted – seconds, minutes – it was outside time. God, in his mercy, did not prolong it. In equal measure to the glory of his coming was the abandonment of his going. Man can sustain neither for more than minutes in this life. It was taken from me as instantaneously as He had gone. Suddenly, like a tidal wave, joy struck me. It crashed into my mind, a great breaker driving sorrow out as it flooded in, flinging the froth of joy in all directions. I was filled, brimful and overflowing, with the most intense, deep, unspeakable joy; I was ablaze with it. It was not joy welling up from within me – it came to me from without; it was given. It was the Spirit of Joy, the Holy Spirit, crashing into, pouring into, flooding my soul, strong, powerful, supreme, ecstatic joy, grasping me and lifting me right out of myself.

The joy of the Spirit is pure gift. It has no rational cause: my joy came from no reasoning of mine, no sensation. Whilst I was still in the aching void of the loss of the God who had been there, sunk in despair, a stranger to hope, Joy burst open the doors of my soul, cascading in, deluging me, lifting me up and flinging me towards heaven, from whence it came. My joy was the Joy that is Spirit. And with the gift of the Spirit came understanding – of what had happened – and increased joy. Not only did God exist, more concretely, more surely than any earthly object, but he loved me. Nothing could make me doubt it; his touch had been a caress; it was unmistakable. And not only did God love me, but I *knew* God. I knew the quality of his love, not because I had been told or even because it was revealed in Scripture, but because I had *experienced* it. He had made himself known, partially lifting the veil of the sacrament and ravishing me with the gentleness, the tenderness, the condescension of the love with which he came. It was divine love incarnate, human love deified. It is the *humanity* of Christ that melts the soul it touches – those qualities we know so well become divine, the Divine become human. No one could feel and be aware of that touch and resist it. It is the touch of the Divine Essence, pure Love, a love revealing itself with such excess that nothing could withstand it. It transforms what it touches, the old form melting and a new emerging prostrate at the feet of the Love that has brought it into being. I knew that Jesus loved me and that that love would never change. He had loved me, and would continue to do so, for all eternity. That knowledge brought total peace, erasing every vestige of sorrow.

My immediate reaction on leaving church was to hide myself away. There was an attic at the top of the house. I longed to go there, to be there alone and, without interruption, to meditate upon and savour the wonder of what had happened. But, just as during the crises of the past I had carried on as usual, hiding the turmoil within, so did I now have to carry on as usual, hopefully masking the miracle of transformation that had taken place. I did not want to eat, but I had to – the boys were there and I had to cook and keep house for them as usual. That evening, to celebrate my reception, G. had booked seats for a concert at the Albert Hall. I did not want to go; no music, however sublime, could match the music in my heart. But I could not disappoint him. All I heard was the crashing of the canons in the 1812 Overture. I was somewhere else. I had been transported to another region; I had entered a new world and I lived in a new dimension.

Chapter 2

I did not go to Mass or Communion during the following week. Deep in my heart I knew it would not be the same next time, nor any other time. The Word had been spoken; there was nothing more to say. His coming and the sending of the Spirit constituted the totality of redemption. I had watched as redemption was enacted within me. The whole doctrine of the Church was enshrined in what had happened: He had been in the consecrated element before I had received it, making his presence known not only at the moment of reception, but before as well; He *was* the Host, the consecrated element not only had no substance, but from the moment of contact it had no accidents either. There was nothing but Him – the Real Presence. He had crossed my threshold, entered in, oned me with himself – and gone. It was all, except for the immediate disappearance of the accidents, exactly in accordance with the Church's doctrine on the Eucharist, affirming it step by step. [Catechism of the Catholic Church (Chapman, 1994) nos. 1374–77; Mysterium Fidei (CTS Do. 355, 1965), nos. 44–7; cf. Francis Clark, A 'New Theology' of the Real Presence (CTS Do. 396, 1969).] Then, true to his promise, He did not leave me long desolate; He sent another Comforter, the Holy Spirit, as his abiding presence. It was all there; love had been declared; all had been said. [John. 14:16–18, 16:7.]

And, indeed, when I did go again the next Sunday, nothing extraordinary happened. But, walking back afterwards, again together with G. and N., suddenly, as if it had been poured into me, I was hit with the knowledge that *I loved God*, completely and utterly, hopelessly lost to him, and for the first time my heart went up to him in an act of pure love: 'My God I love you.' I was *in* love with God. The realisation had come in an instant, more sharply defined than could be the case in natural love; to me at any rate, falling in love naturally had been a gradual process. This was pure gift from God, given in an instant, whole, perfect and complete. It no more originated from me than did anything that had happened the previous Sunday: only the response was mine, the lifting up and going forth of the heart, towards God its Beloved, in its very first act of love. Perhaps the joy and astonishment of this were even greater than that of his coming. We are told, we have the evidence of Scripture, of God's love for us; when he manifests it, it is its extent and quality that overwhelm and astonish us. We are told that we must love God, but this remains an abstract act of the will, manifested in obedience to his commands; we might perhaps hope for, or even achieve, a feeling that God is a friend, but beyond this we would not dare to go – anything more would be attained only in the next life. This, at any rate, was my thinking, with its austere Protestant conditioning and total ignorance of Catholic devotions. I did not even know that a *possibility* of anything else existed for me. The effect, then, of knowing in an instant that I loved God, that I had fallen in love with him in the same way that human beings fall in love with each other, only with an infinitely greater intensity, was shattering, the joy inebriating and indescribable. God had become a lover, and inwardly I entered into the most intimate association of love. From that moment my adoration was centred on the Eucharistic Christ; I was totally his; I was lost to Him.

Afterwards I realised the extraordinary fittingness of God's designs, and how this was the fruit of the sacrament of penance. At my first Confession the penance given to me was to say ten times: 'My God I love you.' This I did many more than ten times, but knowing full well it meant nothing to me. Much as I would have liked them to mean something, I knew they were empty words. I knew I did not love God – not in the way that I understood love.

My reactions to Our Lord's coming that Sunday was one of utter amazement. I had no concept of the possibility of such an event. Being prepared for my first Communion as a Protestant, I had been told specifically never to expect to feel anything, and nothing had been said in my instructions to contradict that. I had no knowledge or notion of any supernatural phenomena of any kind, other than dreams of the Evil One, and would, in any case, have thought any divine intervention belonged to the time of the early saints and was no longer even a possibility. Things like Lourdes were an unknown quantity to me; I was somewhat sceptical and very ignorant of all things Catholic, other than doctrine, of which by then I had a good grounding. I had gone to receive my Saviour in pure faith; I knew nothing, I wanted nothing, I expected nothing – except eternal life. The shock of God emerging as a reality, more concrete than any human person or material object, was like being hit over the head with a sledge-hammer. It was the difference between believing and knowing. I had always believed that God exists, but the utter unexpectedness when he actually emerged as a living reality was devastating. I was stunned and for years reeled from the shock. In fact, one never entirely recovers, but bears the wound for ever.

It was as if a guillotine had dropped upon my life, cleanly severing and cauterising the festering limb of the past. The gaping wound was healed, only the scar remained, a testimony to suffering, suffering which God had transformed, but the events of which even he could not undo. From that moment there has never been a twinge of pain from it; there is no past to hurt; A. and everything to do with him was handed over to Our Lord as I breathed my prayer to Him. He took it from me to himself, as He said he would: 'Your sorrow shall be turned to joy . . . and your joy no man shall take from you.' [John. 16:20, 22.]

He took the pain and He took the guilt, and He transformed them; not only the past, the present too. As He melted into me, suffering dissolved into Him and was given back to me, in himself, as love and joy, and guilt came back as peace. That grief has never returned, nor can grief or sorrow about anyone or anything wound as before. Insight and empathy for the sorrows of others is deeper, but the sting has gone, the backlash is minimal. There is nothing that can disturb this 'peace that passes understanding', this joy in the Risen Christ, because his love is *known* to be softer, tenderer, gentler, more merciful than all the hardness, pain and sorrow in the whole world; He has conquered death, they have no more power. I know the end; He is the end; and I know Him and have 'seen' Him. It is as if, whilst in the middle of a book, I had read the end. I know the end. I cannot lose that knowledge and I cannot forget it, and no one can take it from me. It is a happy, blessed end, and so I am no longer able to shed tears over the book. He is the end for me and for others; and on the way all things, suffering and distress, mine and others', are transmuted in that End. Dying was the prelude to his coming. Afterwards death has no more power – you have died and Christ has raised you up into a new type of existence from which the sting of suffering has been excised. There is no longer any past of *any* sort – because I cannot look behind; I cannot withdraw my gaze from the Beauty to which it is riveted. What happened yesterday, even were it a most unusual event, immediately slips into oblivion unheeded. It is gone, almost without my knowing it had ever been. There is no past, and only one future – death, and death is only the difference between God now and God then. Time is meaningless. It is so long since He came, and yet so short a time; death is so long coming, and yet it will be here so soon with so much still to do. There is nothing between these points, except 'God now'. There is nothing to refer back to, and nothing to anticipate, because nothing can have more relevance than God, and God can never have more relevance for me than now, at this minute. God is eternal, but he moves with me through time. He fulfils my every instant. He is not more in any yesterday, even the yesterday of his Coming, because he fulfils my being today. He is not more in any tomorrow, because I cannot exceed the fullness of my being.

Tomorrow my potential may grow, in which case he will fill that potential, so that still he will be the fullness of my being. Always it is so. Only death stands out as the beginning of a new potential and relationship. Events and details of every sort, having imposed their stamp on 'now', have no more relevance and pass unheeded out of sight. You go on living in the world, but you are not of it, you are halfway between earth and heaven. Everything about you is different, even your body, your relationship with everyone else, with nature, with the whole cosmos. There is no fear, only the warmth and softness and gentleness of God – all around you, in the air you breathe, in the house, outside the house, wherever you go or wherever you are. It is like inhaling God, breathing, peace.

Mind was left lagging far behind senses and heart. The senses instinctively knew the source of the sweetness that assailed them, the heart was captivated and surrendered, but the intellect beheld the abyss of mystery and blindly groped to correlate the mighty impact of faith become fact. The knowledge Our Lord gave at his coming was blinding. Only as time went on did I begin to see the extent of that

93

knowledge, which penetrated deeper day by day. It was as if the whole basis of theology had been imparted in the few minutes of his presence. So blinding was the light and the knowledge that it could not begin to be assimilated, and so began a ceaseless struggle for conceptualisation. The instantaneous transition from belief to knowledge is so overwhelming and so stunning that the mind is unable to reorientate itself. Possibly this is one of the reasons why, when this happens, God so inebriates the person with joy and peace that the mind is incapable of thought. It does not have to do anything, because God seizes it and has control of it; it is passive in his hands. If this were not so, some injury would be done to it but, during this period, when the person lives in a state of almost constant rapture, dizzy with joy, the mind is able to begin to adapt itself to the shock, to which there can be no equal.

Like a schizophrenic, I lived in two different worlds. I was shot into the timeless world of spirit, where God initiated me, enticing me with unimaginable delights. Transfixed and enraptured, I wanted to remain constantly in that region, but I had to continue my ordinary everyday existence. I could not abandon my job. N. was still at school. I had to continue to earn a living and keep the home going. Every moment that my mind was not forcibly occupied with other matters, it would revert like the needle of a compass to the God who was exerting such delicious pressure. Consciously caught and held in his grasp, intoxicated with awareness of the movements of grace, I had to force myself to be absolutely ordinary, allowing no hint of it to escape into my behaviour. This wound of split personality never completely heals. As with the passing of time God withdraws the carrot of spiritual delight and the acute awareness of his presence begins to dim, so the two worlds become more compatible until the supernatural is, as it were, imposed on the natural. Then one does not have to inhabit another region to find God; all things speak of him and manifest his presence. But it is still not enough; it is not total possession; it is only a shadow of the longed-for consummation of the other world; life is but a waiting for death.

On leaving church my first thought had been: so this is the Catholic Eucharist; this must happen to everybody. Perhaps, I thought, it was something that happened just once in a person's life, maybe at first Communion. But I had never heard any mention of it, and my sons had never given any indication. I decided that, because it was such a sublime secret, no one ever spoke of it, but all knew of it and fed on it in their hearts. Before I arrived home, I knew it was not so. I already knew it endows the recipient with benevolence, with which certain things are immediately recognisable as incompatible, notably any disorientation from God and any flavour of uncharitableness towards others. I thought of how people sometimes behaved inimically to one another, even directly after receiving Communion, and I know the two things were totally incompatible. It bothered me, because if it did not happen to everyone, then why had it happened to me? It never occurred to me to question the authenticity of the event. With the event was given the knowledge of its origin; it was self-authenticating. It *was* the Eucharist; it was the hidden reality made manifest to my awareness. What was extraordinary was the gift of awareness. I had to find a priest, not to ask *whether* it had been Our Lord, but whether this happened to everyone at some time in their lives. My question was: does Our Lord always make himself known in the Eucharist?

For months I searched the face above every dog collar, wondering if I would find a priest I could tell. The one who had received me had been ill and unobtainable, but eventually I ran him to earth in the confessional and put my question, without any supporting details. His response was to query whether it had not been imagination. This, of course, is the first point a wise confessor would want to eliminate, but to me then the mere suggestion that this stunning, world-shattering event could be put down to imagination made me feel we were talking different languages. I did not want corroboration of the event, but an answer to my question: does Our Lord always make himself known in the Eucharist – does He make his presence felt to everyone at some time or other? I knew the conversation was not meant to be prolonged, and could only tell him it could not be imagination because 'I never knew such things could be.' Of course he was quite right in his attitude: he did not know what I was talking about, I had not told him anything, and for all he knew the experience of Christ's presence which my question implied might well have been a figment of the imagination. It was God telling me to wait: it was not the *kairos*, not his time. Exactly a year after his coming, God led me to a priest who answered my question in full.

For a year I had never spoken about it to anyone or given any indication of what had happened. God alone was my guide: God the Holy Spirit dwelling within me. In the coming of the Risen, Glorified Christ and the sending of the Holy Spirit, I had been re-created. It took time for the realisation and significance of this to penetrate: the Holy Spirit had to teach me how to live as my re-created self. Immediately he began to teach me to mortify my appetites. If I picked up a biscuit, a compulsion made me drop it back in the tin. It was the same with everything, cakes, biscuits, sweets, hot drinks at night were all cut out. It extended to meal times, less was eaten and all inessentials cut out – unless others were present; I limited myself to a very meagre mid-day meal. At the same time, fasting was made easy and had no effect on me so that, if necessary, or if I was working at night, I could go hours without food. I would often get up in the morning, walk two miles to Mass at the Abbey and on to the office, where four hours after I had got up, I would break my fast with four digestive biscuits when the coffee came round at ten o'clock. Sometimes I was extremely hungry, but God gives grace so that it has no effect. Previously, if I had had less than usual at lunch-time, by the time I got home in the evening I would be shaking from need of food. Such symptoms entirely disappeared, even when I felt desperately empty; in fact I began to prefer to be a little empty: I was physically incapable of eating what I used to. I knew nothing about mortification, I hardly knew what the word meant. It was entirely the work of the Holy Spirit applying a very strong and irresistible compulsion. I only knew that I must obey the strong, clear, interior prompting. At the same time the will cooperated and set itself on maintaining what it had been taught.

My whole psyche was invaded by that sweet, gentle power; there was a subtle change in every relationship with the world and everything in it. Where before I had displayed acute irritation and often uncontrollable anger at any provocation, now I was, as it were, insulated with the unction of the Holy Spirit, and able to endure in perfect peace and without a twinge of asperity situations which previously would have caused me to fly into a rage. Yet the effect was far more deep seated and subtle than this; it was one of total reconciliation, a barrier, which I had not realised existed between me and other people, was dissolved. This even had physical aspects. Previously I had found it offensive to have to sit so close to a stranger that there was physical contact. Now it was as if the sweet softness of the interior disposition exuded into my flesh, cushioning it; a soothing oil, a balm, dispensed internally, spreading all over my body to the outer extremities, so that no exterior circumstances, other than direct physical injury, could penetrate or cause disturbance. I remember how the full significance of what was happening came home to me as I stood in the check-out queue in Sainsbury's. Someone must have banged into me or pushed in front of me in the queue. I clearly registered my lack of reaction: I *ought* to have been irritated. But I wasn't, there was no effect at all, just the same, undisturbed, sweet, happy, gentle peace within. I had done nothing, made no effort, no act. So it was with everything. I was entirely under the sway of the Holy Spirit.

I was ruled by the Holy Spirit in unity, order, simplicity. He taught me the elements of poverty, chastity and obedience. I no longer wanted anything for myself, instead I found I wanted to give, particularly to the poor; I had a great repugnance at having to buy anything for myself. He did not teach me, so much as bestow chastity, following an occasion which could have proved dangerous, but into which I went armed with much prayer. The change in my sexual reactions which took place had its origin neither in my efforts – which would be powerless to effect a change, because we cannot alter nature – nor in nature itself. Nature was active one minute, and laid to rest the next, habitually (but, as I have always realised, only so long as my will cooperates) – and only the Holy Spirit can accomplish this. He taught me obedience to the Church in wanting to read and learn only from the approved sources, rejecting what was not in this category and, in fact, reserving my intellect wholly for himself by making it impossible for me to apply it to *any* secular material other than the obligations of my work. At this time my spiritual ignorance was total. As a Protestant I had been taught nothing of the spiritual life, only to worship God in spirit. I was not told that I could hope for an intimate relationship with God in this life, a real relationship, a love relationship. I had read many books on Catholicism, some theology and apologetics, but no spiritual books with the exception of some of Thomas Merton, and those not recently. The Holy Spirit alone taught me the basis of the spiritual life and even its application. For about six weeks, in this respect, my soul was absolutely virgin to the hand of God. Then natural curiosity got the upper hand, the tree of knowledge was plucked when I began to read – first St. Teresa's *Way of Perfection* then *The Cloud of Unknowing*. Perhaps this is the point at which the acute awareness of the action of God within began very gradually to recede: the innocence of the spirit had been touched by human intervention; it was no longer virgin soil tilled only by God.

I found that, with the dissolution of the invisible barrier between me and others, physical revulsion had likewise been transformed. People I would previously have found repellent or conditions which would have made me retch no longer had any effect. I had a deep empathy with and respect for the sufferer, whom I saw as specially graced and loved by God. It was not that I was indifferent, but I saw suffering in the light of eternity with an understanding deeper than any emotive quality. Since his coming there have been many trials, severe tensions and difficulties but, however uncongenial the conditions, never a moment's boredom. Boredom is not compatible with the fullness within, which is always there to turn to. There has never been a 'Monday morning', because Christ lives in every day, every day is God's day.

I felt full of the Holy Spirit, stunned with the newness of my transformed state. I felt completely forgiven, reconciled in friendship, and more, in loving intimacy with God. I felt shining white, as if I wore a beautiful white garment and as if, were I to run my hand down my front, I would feel it or, casting my glance down, would be dazzled by its whiteness. I seemed to be all Holy Spirit and nothing but Holy Spirit. My mind was completely under his action, inebriated with joy, my body too was under his control, all things being ordered in softness and sweetness. I was no longer my own; I had been invaded and taken over by the Spirit, and what had been me stood back and watched, amazed and aghast, fearful lest I undo or interfere with that work of the Spirit. The realisation that, although none of it was my doing, I could, by a sinful act, lose it all yawned like a great cavity at my feet. The very thought of sin of any kind, of falling away from God, of losing or in any way interfering with the blessed state of union which he had bestowed appalled me. I felt I was walking along the edge of a precipice. So much had been given, there was so much to lose; the good was not mine, the ability to commit sin and forfeit the gift was. If that happened, I would know his going, just as I had known the going of Our Lord. It was not just that this effect of grave sin was too awful to be thought, but that I wanted never to sully in the slightest the relationship which God in the abundance of his merciful goodness had established. I was filled with fear of sin to the extent that I was filled with love of God.

So bemused was I at this new dimension I had entered that at first I became very absent-minded and a menace to myself. On one occasion I removed the guard from an electric fire and dusted it whilst it was on and wondered at the odd sensation in my little finger which was up against the element. On another, I shattered a hot electric light bulb through wiping it with a damp cloth, and on yet another almost walked under a car at a pedestrian crossing, so that the car and I both stopped at the same moment as its mudguard was up against my coat and its wheel about to run over my toes. These are things I would never have done previously, and in each case I was lost in thought – buried in God, who protected me from harm.

Chapter 3

The lone tutoring by the Holy Spirit continued for a year. I never spoke to anyone about it nor gave any indication of what was happening. God alone was my guide, God the Holy Spirit dwelling within me. And the most persistent and deeply impressionable of all his teaching was that on prayer.

Within a matter of days, or a week at the most from his coming, I was left entirely alone at home, both boys being elsewhere occupied during the long vacation which was just beginning. I had to do my best to continue to be efficient in my work, but in the solitude of the house I was taken somewhere I had never been before nor even knew existed: the realm of prayer. Up to the time of my reception, although I had always been eager to attend church services and listen to sermons, personal prayer had been a trial, a dutiful ten minutes a day to be got through as quickly as possible. From the moment I returned to the house that first Sunday, God started to teach me to pray. In the evenings or at the week-end, whilst I went about my household tasks, I would find myself standing still, my hands joined together, palms touching, fingers pointing upwards, an attitude I had never adopted before. Whenever I was alone at home, or there was no one in the room and I was not actively engaged, my hands arrived in that position. I used to find myself walking around the house like that; if I sat down or fell into meditation whilst reading they were always in that attitude: or I would find myself, hands together, gazing out of the window in a semi-trance. I would become transfixed, carried away by the Spirit, so that the world dropped away from me as I entered this new-found spiritual dimension.

I don't know how long I would remain like that, I suppose for anything from ten to thirty minutes. I was far too lost to realise what was happening. Only afterwards did its significance become apparent. Again and again the Holy Spirit had placed my hands in the attitude of prayer. During those first weeks I was in an habitual state of rapture, snatched right out of myself. It was a thing of the mind. Every moment when my attention was not specifically diverted by some action, my mind went leaping to God. It was an upward thrust, a rushing of the mind to God, a soaring of the whole being to God, acutely felt in the mind, causing a rapture of delight, occurring again and again for weeks and weeks, gradually diminishing in intensity.

Straightaway I began allotting time for prayer at night. At first there was just the sheer delight of re-living and basking in the experience of his coming. But within a few days God started to intervene again, alluring me with indescribable delights; it was no longer a matter of re-creating his vast presence, but of savouring a new prayer-presence. The moment I knelt and closed my eyes, God was there, actually present, making his presence known and felt, but in a more inexpressible and intangible manner than in his Eucharistic coming. It was a presence which only came when I was in a traditional praying attitude – on my knees with my eyes closed. So vivid and so sweet was it that at home I would kneel down over and over again during the day to make sure it was still there. I could not believe it would last: I felt it must disappear. When I was not on my knees I was like a little child who has strayed from its mother and runs back to make sure she is still there: I had to keep going back to my knees to see if God was still there. And, like a mother solicitous for her little one as it takes its first faltering steps, he was always there waiting for me.

Quite soon came the first of the three or four occasions that God drew me right up into himself. When this happened there seemed to be two different actions going on at the same time, one on the body and the other on the soul, although it was actually one and the same action. The first intimation was a feeling of relaxation throughout my limbs, as if I were held up without any support from myself and, at the same time, a feeling spreading throughout my body which can only be described as that of perfect health – so perfect that it is supernatural. If I was kneeling supported, I changed to an upright position, the better to receive God, who I knew was coming. I would become locked in that position. These three or four ecstasies did not come suddenly, they came gradually, delectably stealing over the body, until it was finally seized. There was a singing in my ears, as if I were going to faint but, whereas fainting is accompanied by unpleasant sensations, this is the opposite. The sensations become sweeter and sweeter until the body is overpowered by them, locked in them; it cannot bear them. At the same time something else is happening to the soul; God has drawn it up into himself. God is a point, and the soul has been drawn into that point. That point is God and God stretches beyond that point to infinity, but in all infinity there is only God and the soul. God draws the soul into himself, deep into the darkness of that point, the depth of that point. In the deep darkness of that point the soul, in delight and rapture which no words can denote – whilst the body is behind on earth bound by the overflow of the soul's rapture – is drawn right into the centre of God to become one with him. It is blended with him, it is one with its Beginning, it has come back to its Last End. There is only knowing and feeling. The soul knows where it is, it knows

103

what is happening; it knows it is in God, it knows this is what it was created for. 'I' is absorbed, blended, melted into God, in God, indistinguishable from God, the only part of 'I' that is not God is knowing and feeling, because if 'I' were all God, there would be neither knowing nor feeling. The soul *feels* all this – it is more than sweetness, it is unbearable in its intensity and it is this unbearableness overflowing into the body which causes its ecstasy. There are no words on earth to describe it. I know not whether the knowing causes the ecstasy, or the ecstasy the knowing; the knowing is the ecstasy, and the ecstasy the knowing, they are inextricably interwoven because what we know in ecstasy is God, and God is the cause of the ecstasy and of the knowing. It seems as if there were two ecstasies, one of the soul, the other of the body, because the soul seems to have gone where the body cannot follow, yet they are one and the same. Soul and body each fulfil their own function, the soul knows, the body feels, but their natural operation is reversed; it is no longer senses feeding the intellect, but the intellect feeding the senses. The soul *knows* God, and is ravished, the body *feels* that ravishment and is caught up in ecstasy.

God returns the soul to earth gradually, so as not to shock it too severely. It comes back as if it had been a long way away, and the body returns to itself. For me this was always to a terrible pounding of the heart, as if it were fighting for its very life, almost bursting through my ribs. I suppose it was struggling to restore the circulation. This was the only unpleasant symptom I had, and at the time it became a little alarming. When it had died down, I was left prostrate in adoration, bathed in happiness and peace, bedewed with the fragrance of God, which seemed to cling about me.

This happened three, or four, times with this terrific intensity. Our Lord came on 14th July and one of these occasions was in September, when I was staying in Cumberland, where I had been so shamed twenty years earlier and, as far as I remember, a week later when I was staying with a friend in Scotland with whom I had been very close years before at school. There was at least one previous occasion at home, and many more similar but of much less intensity.

Eventually God banished me. He came as a ball of fire, suddenly, straight towards me and at me. The ball of fire reached me and vanished, and God was upon me. He was neither before, nor behind, nor beside, nor above, but *upon* me, all around me, everywhere. He was upon me with all his omnipotence and, in that moment, I knew and understood his might and his all-powerfulness – and I was afraid and shrank. He went; I was left shivering, and the fear of God was put into me. It was as if he had said: 'You have been too near; go back.'

After that, he still came, but never so intensely; he started gradually to withdraw the delights of these visits. I weakened. Although I was not actually afraid, the terrible pounding of my heart when I came back to myself was so unpleasant that I asked God to ease it.

This union with the Godhead is different and more intense than the union with the Eucharistic Christ. Our Lord comes as God made man, risen and glorified, with human attributes, deified, so soft, so gentle so tender. He melts over the threshold of our flesh, his vibrant glory, muted to our weakness, spreading within our body. It is his *body* with which we are filled, and with his body all of Him, but his body is not like ours, it is a risen, glorified, spiritual body. In the union with God the Father there is no body. He has no body, and the soul, when plunged into the heart of the Godhead has no body. In the union with God the Son, there is acute consciousness of the body and the glory with which it is filled. In the union with God the Father, although the body is so affected by what is taking place that it is seized and held in ecstasy, at the same time the soul, drawn and plunged into the vortex that is God, has no knowledge of its body. It is the spirit that is made one with God the Father, who is spirit; and the oneness and absorption are so great that all that is left is knowing and feeling. All else has been drawn into God, melting into his oneness. There is no desire to 'see' God, for this is more than seeing, it is a state of being. To 'see' we must stand apart and look, either with our eyes or our intellect, but this is to know God by being submerged and transformed into him, so that all has become him, save only knowing. This knowing is not observing, for all that could have observed or been observed has been lost and fused into God. It is simply *awareness*, pure, white-hot awareness, an awareness that, in one perfect and continuous act, appreciates its oneness and absorption in God. We came from God, thought in the mind of God and created, and we are drawn back into the heart of God whose love gave us life, has sustained and brought us back to our true home, our only satisfaction.

Once the soul has been thus united with God, there is no other satisfaction; nothing else exists for it in heaven or on earth. It becomes literally an exile living in an alien world; no beauty can touch the one who has been touched by God; no angel, saint in heaven or person on earth can give anything to one who has known God, no emotion can arouse those who have been made one with God. This is not to say they cease to love, that they cannot learn humanly from others, that others may not be more virtuous, that they do not seek ceaselessly to acquire more knowledge of God from every source available – but what more can anyone tell those to whom God has manifested himself? God cannot give himself in part and to whomsoever he manifests himself, he does so whole and entire. Anyone to whom God has given himself, possesses all of him, undivided. Therefore, no one can add to this possession and, in the God whom we possess, already exists all that anyone else can give us. The whole of God lies latent within us, and it is by turning inward to contemplation of the divinity within that we shall learn more of him. Incapacitated in the current of that divine love, the soul is drawn like a steel shaving towards the magnet. It drops all, forgets all, following the irresistible and irrevocable call which, once heard, forever echoes: 'Come away, my beloved, come away.' [Song of Solomon. 2:10, 13.] It strives always towards God, goaded by a love that is merciless, that gives no respite, but wherein lies the measureless rest and peace that is God.

With the gradual abatement in intensity of awareness of God's presence, I entered a new state of prayer, different from that which had gone before when God had taken all the action, snatching the soul to himself. Now I tried to take action myself; I started to work very hard at my prayer. Somehow I knew what God wanted me to do: I had to wait in silence and emptiness for his coming, and my work was the emptying of myself. For one new to prayer, this was very difficult. It required supreme concentration, an intense turning inward, deeper and deeper, emptier and emptier. I knew I must be empty to receive God – at the same time the Holy Spirit ensured that on the material level my mind absorbed nothing that was not essential to my duties. From the very beginning, to me this seemed an essential of this type of prayer and, most important of all, there must be no trace of imagination. I realised the danger of imagination in this area, and rejected it completely, which meant giving it no material to work on, no 'entertainments' of any kind, no secular books or magazines, the very minimum of news-papers, no radio – at first a few religious broadcasts and symphony concerts, then nothing for months and months. As far as the things of God were concerned, I allowed myself to remember what had happened, but I tried not to dwell too much on its sweetness, because I knew I must not remain there; it had only been a beginning and I must go forward, even from the events of that first Sunday. I must not hold any such experience to myself, but let it go, hand it back to God, so that he could lead me still further. I never allowed myself any image or consideration of what could or might happen, I shunned any books dealing with visions, as opposed to infused knowledge of God. Apart from the occasion of the ball of fire, there had been no images in God's visits. He had taught me without images and forms to 'feel' his essence, and I knew this was the way he wanted it. So I worked to wait for him in emptiness.

Every day I prayed like that, and almost every day he came to me – not in the previously unbearably intense manner, but in the same way in a modified form. This is almost impossible to describe. After perhaps half to three quarters of an hour of profound concentration on God as a point, a point without shape, form, or any characteristic, just God, a point that is to be found deep, deep inward in the emptiness of oneself, he would come. Again, he would draw me to himself, but much more gently, indefinably sometimes, more intensely at others, until again I became fused with him, was one with him. These touches were much more delicate and, although they filled the soul and the body with delight, they were not of that terrible intensity which binds in ecstasy. Then he would recede and I would be left content and happy, lingering in prayer. This went on for months and months.

It seemed to me that, whereas when the will is conformed to God, one can be in a state of union with him at all times, prayer is the *act* of union. There lingered at the back of my mind an analogy regarding the frequent, but less well-defined visits, in which there seemed to be a very delicate parallel with the act of union between man and woman in the natural sphere. There was a time of waiting and preparing for the Beloved, there was the time of his arrival – he was known to be there, he had entered the room – there was the enjoyment of his sweetness, the time of making love;

there was a time of attaining towards a climax, not reached at once, but as it were by degrees, each degree nearer than the last. As it is in physical love, so it was in this prayer that the soul strove to reach fruition in God, but could not quite attain it immediately, even after he had come; it seemed to come nearer and nearer, until there came a point where God bent down and lifted the soul into himself, so that it had perfect fruition (corresponding to the climax in physical love). Then he gradually withdrew, leaving the soul in perfect happiness and contentment (as the body is left after the physical act). This analogy is entirely spiritual, very delicate and difficult to convey.

At first I rejected it as being unfitting. Then I thought: why should it be? God created the union between man and woman, and the more one learns of the spiritual, the more one realises the parallel of the natural. They are miraculously interwoven. The natural union is but a faint shadow mirroring the supernatural union of the soul with God. God comes to each person in the way most suited to them, he speaks their language. To me he has always come as a Lover and, if for me the union has this shade of meaning, again it is because it is something I understand. Although there are states of prayer, union, ecstasy common to all those who are called to them, the descriptions of which can be recognised, there is also a nuance individual to each person. It is the same God who comes to all, but that coming is adapted to the capacity and vocation of the individual.

It was thus God taught me to pray. He even taught me how long. Always I had to wait thirty to forty-five minutes before he came. My part was to be empty, waiting, ready to receive him. There was nothing I had to do, or indeed could do, except sweep away the dust and rubble of mental activity, anxiety, attachments, whatever could constitute a hindrance to his coming. He only comes in this way when we have let go of everything else and set our heart's eye on him. He is our fullness, but there must first be emptiness. Ever since, I have tried to pray this prayer, setting the whole power of my concentration on him alone, with various degrees of success, for an hour a day, usually in one unbroken session but divided into two if circumstances necessitate. This is the prayer I *must* pray, because it is the prayer <u>God taught me</u>. It demands a relentless obedience; it is a command of God which I dare not ignore. There are no extenuating circumstances, other than incapacitating illness. Whilst I can stand on my feet, nothing excuses me from this prayer because it is imposed by God himself. It has gone through many stages since then; mostly it is a joy but sometimes there have been severe obstacles and it has required great determination to be faithful. Yet it is never a burden, the yoke is light. It is not difficult to be faithful; I cannot help myself, because love is faithful. It is love which drives me to be faithful to what I see as a command of God which has never been rescinded. Nor could I live without this prayer; together with the Eucharist, it is the unifying force of my being and the source of all my vitality. Without it I would disintegrate.

For several years the pull to prayer was so strong that it was never a matter of having to make an effort to pray, but of having to accommodate to an attraction that was almost irresistible. This terrific magnetism directed my way through all the early trials which soon came. My longing, of course, was for silence and solitude, but there were many family commitments and frequent comings and goings. I remember, during the long vacations, when N. was down from Oxford, being hounded from room to room by him and his transistor, from which he was then inseparable. Wherever N. went, his transistor went. I would be praying, when I would hear them approaching, and would quickly get up from my knees. After a little while, the pull would be too strong for me and I would make some excuse to go off into another room to continue my prayer where, as likely as not, the pair would soon pursue me. Probably the transistor was filling a gap on the part of what must have been a very strange and unsatisfying parent. Just as with a human love affair, I was extremely careful to hide what was going on and not be caught in an attitude of prayer, other than by my bed at night where it was to be expected. It was not only that, although I knew I was now odd by the world's standards, I did not want to appear odd, but that my prayer life, which expressed my union with God, was too sacred for any eye to behold; it was sacrosanct. It had to remain veiled and hidden.

Chapter 4

There was also the problem of driving my body beyond its natural capacity. Within two to three years my commitments had greatly increased and, including two to two and a half hours' prayer a day, I was leading an eighteen-hour day, almost every day, with perhaps two hours less on Sundays. My days were often so concentrated that there was no turning aside for as much as five minutes. Sometimes I would be typing for hours after I got home at night, sometimes in the evening I would help at Servite House and one evening a week for three years I attended a theology course at Westminster. This, with an hour's prayer before the Blessed Sacrament, was the highlight of the week. My recreation was spiritual reading at meal times – but the real recreation was prayer. It did not matter how late it was when I had finished or when I got home, I had to pray. Sometimes when I was most tired or it was very late, when I knelt down God would add to the lateness by binding me to himself so strongly that I would be there far longer than I had intended. Time would lose its dimension and be telescoped into God; an hour or more would be as a few minutes, and it would be impossible to account for what had happened during that time; I only knew I had been with God. On one occasion I knelt down intending to spend not more than half an hour in prayer, and got up two hours later. It was not that I slept; during this period, when God

113

was so active within me, I never slept during prayer; later, sometimes certainly, but not then. The demands of prayer on top of everything else at that time, and many times since, were indeed terrible. Whilst you are in the world you have no protection from its exigencies. There are no boundaries behind which to isolate yourself because you want to pray – prayer has already razed all boundaries. The one who prays must expect to be used by God; as he moulds you in prayer, so he increasingly offers opportunities for sharing in his work, and this means all sorts of unexpected demands and commitments. So, for me, they mushroomed. But none, however heavy, could exempt me from prayer. Love is compelled to offer obedience. I often wondered how long I could go on doing it, and how much grace God would give to make it possible. To lead a life that seeks God with such intense intent and purpose at the same time as a fully active life, demands a driving and discipline of the flesh that is merciless and never ceases. I used to feel as though I were walking along the edge of a precipice – the next demand would push me over – but even if I did fall over, what would it matter, for I would only fall into the arms of God?

Within a few weeks of his original coming, God came to me in another way – in a dream. I dreamed that I stood in the lounge of the house in Ealing where we were then living. I faced the window out onto the street: on my right was the empty armchair in which A. always used to sit. On my left stood a man, also facing the window, but as he was beside me, parallel with me. I did not see his face or know who he was. Outside the window in the street was another man: his appearance was quite ordinary, and I think he stood beside a car. A stream of love radiated between the man next to me and the man standing in the street. The man next to me pointed to the man in the street and said, 'There he is', and I knew he meant that it was Our Lord. I was overcome with acute envy. I envied the man his intense union with Our

Lord, made known to me through the current of love which passed between them. I was outside and excluded from this personal, individual relationship, this stream of love which united them, and was desolate with longing for it. Suddenly, I too was caught up in that current, but it was not that I was included in their relationship. It was my own individual current of love and relationship with Our Blessed Lord. It was *exactly* the same, and yet it was my own personal stream of love. The full force of the love which had united them was now directed at me, enveloping me in delight. It was all mine, as much as it had been theirs. It was exactly what I had envied, the same radiating stream of love, the character and significance of which was understood intuitively, and yet at the same time it was uniquely my own, uniting me alone to Our Lord. We were both individually united to Him, and yet the bond of union was exactly the same. At first I had been extrinsic to the current which passed between the man and Our Lord. I had felt it, understood what it was, but been entirely excluded. Now suddenly, it was mine, my own unique bond of union, my own stream of love connecting me with Our Lord, radiating from Him and drawing me into its magnetic power – whilst at the same time the man beside me was still connected by his current, entirely independent of and exterior to mine. What I now had was the same as that which he had had, and still had; I had wanted it, and now I had it and knew it for my own.

Suddenly, as dreams do, its form changed. I was snatched up into the air, drawn upwards at incalculable speed. It was no longer God the Son, Jesus God and man, who was active, it was God the Father. That stream of love radiating from God the Son had been something vital, active, uniting me with its object in indescribable delight, so that none who saw and understood it could bear to be excluded. The current from God the Father was different, immeasurably more dynamic; it was pure omnipotence exerted on a single soul, drawing it to himself at cosmic speed. Again, it was a lone relationship which seized me, and me alone, in a kind of ecstasy, excluding all else. Yet at the same time the man had been snatched up, too, but there was no consciousness of the other person. All that could be felt was God pulling. God draws man to himself with the most dynamic suction that could ever be imagined; my body was clutched by a force tearing at the entrails, my soul by another part of the same force, tearing at the heart, the head – I don't know, I cannot remember – I only know that there was a double link, body and soul, as it were one current, two wires, one connected to the body, one to the soul. The speed with which I travelled upwards was indescribable, the force of the pull excruciating. At first I struggled, then realised it was useless against a force so irresistible, a magnetism so electric and so tremendous. Powerless, I surrendered to excruciating bliss. Suddenly, without any warning, I was wide awake, completely awake. I knew where I was going: *straight to the heart of God*. I knew with a knowledge that was simple and complete. The words were given: they were not dreamed, they were not spoken, nor heard, nor seen. They were infused, infused in *exact and indelible form* at the moment of waking. They were given in the form of perfect knowledge – not known one moment, and known the next, known absolutely, beyond shadow of doubt, beyond reasoning or any discursive element – and received in the instant of giving, whole, entire and perfect – immutable, the same now as on the day of my dream.

The whole of this dream was entirely supernatural. Such a dream has a unique quality, recognisable to the dreamer. It is like no other. It has a supernatural dimension, which is impossible to describe. It is clear and exact and is branded into the memory. It is distinguishable from any other dream and known for what it is. It is easy to understand why St. Joseph and some of the Old Testament figures responded so

promptly to their dreams. They knew they were from God
– God has ways of authenticating himself. The effect of the
dream and the knowledge of my destination was most
profound and lasting peace and tranquillity, a deep, quiet
joy and renewed surrender to the God who had seized me
for himself. Afterwards I speculated who the man could be
who was travelling with me to God. God has never told me
directly; he left me to draw my own conclusions, which I
did a year later.

I had no other divinely inspired dreams but, as so often
happens in such circumstances, the Devil, not to be outdone,
insinuated himself. All my life I had, from time to time,
experienced the presence of evil in dreams. These dreams
were terrible and terrifying, and they were always the same
in essence: I am in an upstairs room, usually an empty room,
not necessarily the same room each time; I am alone.
Suddenly the light goes out, silently and of its own accord,
and there is darkness. That darkness is evil. There is nothing
in the room, no shape and no form – only the darkness, and
in that darkness abides the very essence of evil. It is spiritu-
ally *felt* with a terror and horror which surpass anything
ever known in the waking or natural order of things, because
it is pure spirit, the Evil One himself. I am filled with
immense repugnance and abhorrence, and yet in some
horrible way the presence draws to itself, it attracts and
magnetises. This is the source of its horror. The terror it
brings is so acute that once in the dream my hair literally
stood up on end. I don't know how it ends, differently each
time I think. Something horrible happens, I struggle and
then I am awake.

I have always known it to be an encounter with the Evil
Spirit. It is unmistakable and known for what it is. All night-
mares are horrible and frightening. This is altogether different, of a different dimension, no longer natural, but supernatural, engendering terror and horror, devastating and

paralysing in effect. It is not evil as a negation of good; nothing negative could provoke such fear and such unbridled terror. This evil is a power, a force. It is a naked spirit-to-spirit encounter with evil. It first came to me when, at about fifteen, I was staying with a school friend. I was very frightened but went to sleep again – and immediately the dream repeated itself exactly. I was then quite terrified. Looking back now, I wonder if it was Satan entering my life at that point. I was not given to lying, but by my silence I had told a mean, cowardly lie. My friend kept horses on which during my visit we hunted a few times. One day we were practising jumps in the field when I fell off. I was not hurt and immediately got on again and continued. At lunch my friend's father said he had seen someone rolling on the grass. There was dead silence. I did not want to own up to the indignity of being the one who had fallen off. My friend gallantly stepped into the breach, saying: 'Oh, it was probably me.' Still I remained silent. Since then the dream came at intervals throughout my life. It has always been essentially the same, although the details vary – always the electric light goes out of its own accord, then the darkness which *is* the evil, and in the absolute emptiness the shapeless, formless presence which can be perceived by none of the five senses, but which is recognised and felt by the soul which recoils in repugnance and horror.

At the time God was teaching me to pray, the Devil came in a different form, but still in dreams. He came once in human form, utterly obscene, such as I had never dreamed nor could have imagined. At the moment of waking I knew with absolute certainty that it was completely Devil inspired. He also came on another occasion in the form of demons – little hands clutching at my throat; horrid, soft little hands with a very light touch, but utterly repulsive. How do I know whose hands they were? That I cannot say, only that the soul knows, and knows with absolute certainty; it does

118

not need to be told. I had a third dream, and this time the Evil Spirit was in my gullet but he had form this time, because he heaved and turned over and went out through my chest – no, not indigestion, nor too much reading about the 'lump' in the 'Cloud of Unknowing', because neither of these can provoke the *knowledge* and the *feel* and the sheer *terror* of the presence of the Devil.

Three years later, in 1966, I had a dream which was worse than anything that had ever gone before, because it ended up with the Devil seizing and entering into me. Again, it was in essence the same as before, although the details were somewhat different. This time I dreamed that as I left the office after work, one side of Ealing was brightly lit up and the other direction was in darkness – not the very black darkness, as was usual in the dream, but an unnatural darkness, not like night and not like fog, but in between the two. I got onto a bus and went into the darkness, and the darkness penetrated into the bus and, as always, it was evil, it was heavy with evil. Then I was suddenly back just outside the office, but in a pub which stands on a corner. There were a lot of people inside, but nothing else and no furniture. At first there was light and the people were talking, but then the darkness from outside pervaded it, and with the darkness came the evil and the terror and, although there were people there, the shapeless, formless presence was the same, and the appalling tide of fear and revulsion swept over me, as it always does. Then this formless thing picked me out from all the people, grabbed me, seized me and entered right into me, as spirit, in the same way as Our Lord does, and in so doing he lifted me up three quarters of the way to the ceiling, but roughly and horribly, sideways – not as God draws with all the force of the Godhead, all the power of the Creator, all the ecstasy of the Trinity, against which one is utterly helpless and yet filled with glory and delight. He flung me up and I was possessed by him, and all my limbs

119

started to jerk as if in a fit. The terror and horror were worse than I had ever known before; there are no words for them, and nothing to which to liken them, because they do not belong to the natural order. I knew I had to call upon Our Lady, but I could not. Often in a nightmare one wants to scream and cannot, and it is the vocal chords which are paralysed. But it was not my vocal cords, it was my will that was paralysed. The paralysis was in my head, in my brain, in my will; I was in the grip of evil. I was inhabited and possessed by the Devil, and the evil was an emptiness, a nothingness in the will. I had to fight that evil, struggle with it, make the most supreme effort to free myself – all in the will – a timeless blankness, a space, an emptiness, an impotence; overpowered by nothingness, I had to gather every force I possessed to tear myself away from the evil which inhabited and paralysed me. It was the greatest act of the will I have ever made. I do not know what I finally said, it seemed an eternity: Holy Mary, Hail Mary, Blessed Virgin, perhaps just Mary, but the moment it was uttered, the dream was shattered and I was awake.

There is no God when I am in the grip of these dreams, he abandons me to them, and it is as if I did not know him. If I retained the knowledge and memory of him, the terror would not be as it is. I am utterly alone and know no help or consolation. I have to suffer and fight the Devil alone. Even the knowledge that I had to call on Our Lady was no consolation because I did not know why or who she was; I was so in the grip of evil that I could not think, only feel. Although so much more terrible than any previous one, this dream did not disturb me on waking, because God was still abiding in my heart with the same peace. He had been there all the time, and I knew that however appalling the horror of these visitations, Satan could never harm me. I felt not only peace, but a great happiness and satisfaction – as if in fighting against Satan I had served God, as if I had fought *for*

God and had emerged victorious. Of course I had done nothing – I had been delivered from the Evil One by the Virgin Mary. My battle had been to break through the paralysis in which the Devil had imprisoned my will, and cry to her for help.

Since then I have only dreamed once of the Evil One. It was the usual dream, just the empty room, the thick darkness pervaded by the overpowering lure of that abhorrent presence. But this time the dream did not affect me with such intense revulsion and terror, because it was in relation to another person, who was in the room and was the subject of the evil influence. Afterwards I did not, as perhaps I should have done, confront the person to warn them. I did not feel there was sufficient evidence to warrant interference. There was no sense of obligation; an evil dream does not impose obligations, even negative ones, as does a divinely inspired one. However, a great evil which later disrupted that person's life, must already have been initiated when I had the dream.

Of course what was happening to me was simply salvation in Christ, redemption and the beginning of sanctification; what is promised to everyone who sincerely repents of their sins and turns to God. But in entering the Roman Catholic Church I had the inestimable blessing of coming to the *source* of grace, God's instrument for the salvation of mankind, from which redemption wells out to the world. The means, the channels of grace, were there for the taking, in full flood, strong and dynamic; I clutched at them and was saturated in their cleansing, life-giving waters. What was extraordinary, therefore, was not sanctifying grace, but the gift of *awareness*, being permitted to watch all that was happening, perceiving all the movements of grace, even the most delicate. One minute I was ungraced, the next flooded with grace, and I knew exactly the psychology of the two states – before and after. In the before state I was not

121

ungraced in the sense of not being under the influence of grace. It was grace that gently attracted me, a light guiding me over the rocks of the barren years, it was grace that kept me faithful in love, it was grace that compelled me eventually to seek reception into the Church. It was a great grace that I was able to try, although unsuccessfully, to surrender my will to God and to experience him as my friend. Yet all this was exterior grace, technically *created grace*, God acting *upon* me, and at the time I was not aware of it. The devastating shock to the psyche was the sudden transition from created to uncreated grace of which it was the subject; *God himself, uncreated grace*, crossed my threshold and took up his abode *within* me. He was no longer acting upon me, but *in* and *for* me; I was totally taken over by God. All I had to do was to surrender to the sweetly controlling power within and, eased by its unction, act in conjunction with its seductive initiatives. One minute I was disintegrated, at the mercy of my violent reactions, subject to moods, impatient, liable to be critical and aggressive, having strong likes and dislikes, self-centred, often bored, having deep-seated fears, physically and psychologically exhausted. The next minute I was integrated, joyful, profoundly peaceful and tranquil, at one with everyone, almost unrufflable, boredom had gone, aversions had gone, fear had gone, exhaustion had gone, self had vanished into God and could no longer be found. Not only had I done nothing at all to reform, but I had not even begun to think about a programme of reform. I had been taken over and instantaneously transformed by the Holy Spirit whose sweet unction was as oil, lubricating what had been harsh and turbulent, making it smooth and orderly.

So conscious was I of all the movements of grace, that in the first weeks, sometimes even an hour or so after receiving Communion, I would feel its grace flowing through my body, not as on the first day, the presence of Jesus, whose sacramental presence in any case would no longer have been there, but the grace effect. I can remember feeling grace, as it were flowing into the bones of my legs. For months, my mind, my heart, the whole of my being was solely occupied with God. So captivated was I that, during Mass or at prayer, it was impossible to have distractions. It was all done for me, my mind was held, and I went about in a state of bemused abstraction. I would walk miles without knowing how I got from one spot to another. Some days I would walk several miles – up to the Abbey early in the morning for Mass, sometimes back to the Abbey at lunch time or to Ealing Broadway, then after work up to Servite House to spend two or three hours helping. There was no time and no effort involved: I was carried by the impetus of the joy of a mind riveted to God. God was within and it did not matter where I was or what I was doing, he was always there. But at the same time, he was pulling very hard, all the time drawing me to go away to be alone with him, either in prayer or in meditative thought, where I could give him the whole of my undivided attention. That was what I wanted to do, and did at every available minute, but I had to resist it at work and in order to perform other duties. Wherever I was, at work, waiting for an appointment, on the bus, stand-ing in a queue, anywhere, I had only to turn inward to savour the joy and peace of his abiding, unchanging pres-ence. But that joy and peace was not only him – it was me too. All was joy and peace, and eventually I could not tell which was him and which was me. The effort to keep my feet on the ground and perform all my ordinary duties and behave quite normally was almost more than I could accom-plish, but somehow I managed it – at least I presume I did. My one concern was, and always has been, that nothing should be seen or known about what had happened. I never had the slightest temptation to tell anyone or discuss it, other than with my spiritual director. More recently I have questioned whether, in so carefully screening this burningly intense inner life, I was not, in fact, again living a lie. Were my inner and outer selves compatible when my exterior behaviour was such a careful damping of my inner ardour? Do not the saints manifest their interior ardour regardless of the consequences, and is not this the very essence of their integrity? On the other hand, perhaps I *do* have to live a lie, to live a beautiful lie in contrast to and in reparation for the ugly lie of the past. One of the greatest pains of my past life was the fact that I was forced to live a lie in respect of my marriage; I had to pretend to be what I was not. It went very deep, so deep that towards the end, when signing my name, my hand would hesitate on the 'W', the flow always faltering at the beginning of my married name. God provides amazingly fitting ways for us to make reparation and put right our wrongs. Maybe this is the way he wants it – I hope so: before I hid the ugliness, the evil, now I hide the beautiful, the good.

Chapter 5

Before a year was out, I knew I wanted to give my life completely to God, but had no idea how to set about it. I started scanning the vocation advertisements in the Catholic press. I did not dare to believe that I could have a vocation, that God was calling me to the religious life, yet that was what I yearned for – to escape from the demands and distractions of the world in order to be able to devote myself to prayer and praise of God. It was the enclosed, contemplative life that attracted me, although then I knew little of the distinction. Just about this time, Lizzie B., to whom my brother had introduced me whilst I was under instruction and who became my sponsor, asked me to go to a retreat. She had asked me the previous year, but I had declined: it was almost immediately after my reception, too near the two-fold shock of A.'s death and Our Lord's coming. Now I was ready for it, eager to experience this previously unheard of process and the convent in which it was held; bitter was my disappointment when I found I did not have a bare cell with nothing but a bed, chair and crucifix, but quite an ordinary little room, even with a dressing table and a mirror. Lizzie B. had told me she wanted me to attend the retreat because it was being taken by a Servite priest whom she wanted me to meet. He was living in Rome, had been a *peritus* at Vatican II and was a member of the Secretariat for Christian Unity. She described him as a pied piper of souls. It was just before this that I had tentatively questioned the priest who had received me regarding Our Lord's self-manifestation and realised he was not the one to help me. I certainly was not prepared to discuss the matter with some strange priest whom I had never met before. However, I remember telling myself that I must be open to God's initiatives. Lizzie B. had spoken of interviews with the priest. I decided I would make no move to obtain one; if I were allotted one, then I would remain open and see how things went, but I would not initiate anything. As it turned out, I got into this priest's confessional, he asked me a question regarding prayer, and before I knew what had happened, I had told him the main facts about God's coming. The retreat to which Lizzie B. had taken me was a Servite Tertiary retreat, the priest being their director. However, he was also the co-founder of the Servite Secular Institute, in which members live in the world a life totally consecrated to God by the traditional vows of poverty, chastity and obedience assimilated to their secular condition. So did God get me where he wanted me. The priest became my director, took me to the institute retreat very shortly afterwards, and before the end of the year I had started attending their monthly meetings. The path to commitment in the institute was not easy or smooth. My first impression at that retreat was not favourable. At that time secular institutes had not yet found their true identity and were still imitating the religious life. I looked around the drab motley of mostly overweight cardiganed females as we sat in a circle, each one with a piece of sewing, and the frail-looking Servite priest shuffled round greeting each one. This, of course, was recreation modelled on religious lines. I had to muster all my faith to overcome my misgivings; if God had chosen these people who, en masse, seemed so unprepossessing, then they were more than good enough for me and I was happy to be numbered among them. It was enough that they were all special to God.

Although there were aspects of the institute which attracted me – the contemplative streak emanating from the founders, the hermits who had always been part of the Servite way of life and the devotion to Our Lady of Sorrows, so relevant to my past life, it was not, in general, what I had thought of or felt I really wanted. I still yearned to be the other side of the grille, but of course I was not yet free to enter any convent. N. was just going up to Oxford and I would have to provide a home for him for at least another three years. However, I loved the training, many aspects of which were new to me and I enjoyed the company of others who were, or who wanted to be, totally committed to Christ. There was an indefinable aura of mystery and wonder in this process of being chosen by God in this special way and being prepared for the irrevocable step of making the vows. Probably during the time whilst I was in training the institute went through its most active era. There was great emphasis on service and caring, on not indulging spiritual appetites. Meetings took place in the disabled home, where we learned to help in a small way. Several members of the institute worked in the Servite homes, some making it their life's work. These people, frequently under what was very obviously considerable stress from over-work, constituted a constant challenge and veiled threat to my contemplative leanings; I felt obliged, by both charity and obedience, to respond to the considerable demands which were made upon my time for help in one form or another. My continual anxiety was that I would be so subjected to the active stress that it would interfere with my prayer life. As I progressed in training, so my commitments snowballed until I was living an eighteen-hour day, often under great stress. I was afraid I would be instructed to reduce my prayer – and I would be able to give no explanation as to why it might not be what God wanted; all I had ever been able to say was that God had

127

taught me to pray – but I never was. Although institute life did not directly help my prayer, but rather made it more difficult by adding other commitments, I suppose it constituted a trial of fidelity through which God moulded me and made me more pliant to his will.

Three years later, when I was to be interviewed for vows, I still did not know where God wanted me. Now that N. was coming down from Oxford, it would be possible for me to enter an enclosed order, after which I was still hankering. On the other hand, I could not ignore the strange way in which I had been led to the Servites. My only desire was to follow God's will in the matter. But there seemed no way in which to ascertain what this was. No one seemed able to help me or give me clear guidance as to where my vocation lay. It seemed there were indications in both directions. I thought the interview would be the deciding factor; I would either be accepted or rejected for vows, the result being God's will. But, of course, there was no question of accepting an unsure candidate. The person asking for vows must be quite certain it is what they want. Although I was certain enough about vows, I was not certain where I was to make them. So it was all thrown back at me. I was refused and told I could not be accepted until I was quite sure the institute was what I was seeking. I then went through a period of acute distress, struggling in prayer and every other means to find where God wanted me. Eventually I was told to ask God to make it so clear that, however stupid I was, I could not mistake it. He did. I received an indication which was so definite and clear that I could in no way mistake it. He wanted me in the institute. From that moment I have never had an instant's doubt that it is where God wants me. Because of the strong pull in the other direction, had I not gone through such an anguished search, I would never have been sure. As it was, I had perfect peace of mind over it. The pull towards the convent no longer mattered; it was a sweet pain, willingly accepted, because I knew I was where I was meant to be.

Nevertheless, I often felt like a fish out of water. Sometimes there seemed to be a tug-of-war going on, the institute members pulling towards the active, whilst I was pulling towards the contemplative. I looked for indications of others, but never found any, afflicted in the way I was. If there were any, no doubt they were as successful in concealing it as I hoped I was. It took me a very long time to integrate into the group life which I, like many others, found something of an ordeal, particularly when I was expected to contribute. I had no experience whatever of group activities. Perseverance and a long time of hovering on the edge was rewarded by a feeling of total integration, acceptance and belonging. But it did not come quickly or easily.

I made my first vows in August 1967. They could not add anything. I was totally given to God from the moment on the road when I knew I loved him. Vows were a joy to make, a ratification and sealing of my commitment, but they in no way altered my interior disposition. I was already irrevocably vowed to God in my heart, irrespective of any status or way of life. I would be as much, no more and no less, given to God whatever form my life took. I had given myself to him, and a true gift has no strings attached: I had already lost myself to him. If the institute did not add anything in this respect, it enriched me in many other ways, particularly in relationships with other members; it brought me much happiness, taught me many things, enlarged my scope of life and gave me opportunities I would not otherwise have had, bringing out many facets and abilities in me which would have remained latent: above all, it gave me the precious gift of the vows and firm support in living them; it also made my life more complex.

My intellect was always trying to catch up with my heart, which far outstripped it. The more I loved, the more I wanted to know of the object of my love. I read most of the great spiritual classics, but I also had a thirst for solid doctrine, and for a year or two St. Thomas's *Summa* was my breakfast reading. The three-year course of weekly doctrinal lectures at Westminster, in which I delighted, was all grist to the mill. It was as if at God's coming I had *experienced* redemption. It had been enacted within me, felt and observed; it was all there, but unconceptualised. I could only partially express it, and that with much labour. I needed a tool, and that tool was doctrine, what the Church taught. My intellect thirsted for God, it thirsted for what my heart possessed. There was no greater delight than to occupy my mind upon God and the things of God. Just as God had ravished my heart, so to contemplate the unfolding of Catholic doctrine, the conceptualised revelation of God, ravished my intellect. My intellect was as captivated as my heart. It wanted to think about God and only God, all the time, not just a small part of the day as was then only possible. It was N. who sowed the seed. One day he asked me why, when he had come down from Oxford, I did not go up to take a degree. Until then I don't think I had thought about it seriously and would have considered myself too old, but he assured me there were plenty of mature students. Of course there was nothing I wanted to study but theology. Study for its own sake was no attraction, but not only to be able, but for it to be the *duty of my state of life* to occupy my mind solely with God and the things of God, would indeed be the greatest satisfaction that anything less than actually experienced union with God could afford.

N.'s suggestion, which I would never have initiated myself, was as a match to the tinder of my longings. When the suggestion was reinforced by my director and confirmed by the institute, I indeed felt it was God's will for me, and from then on nothing could extinguish the fire that had been set alight. But how to set about studying theology, I had no idea. My director, the only one who might have been able to help, had promptly disappeared back to Rome. I wanted a degree course in *Catholic* theology, *what the Church teaches*. Nothing else would do. I wanted the truth about God – that is, God's self-revelation, enshrined and preserved in his Church, handed on from generation to generation from the beginning until the end of time. What I was seeking was a Catholic university or at least a Catholic faculty of theology. This ruled out all the universities in the British Isles, since in each case they offered only a Protestant divinity degree and, where there were Catholic colleges attached to the universities with Catholic tutors, these did not take women. The only possibilities seemed to be Louvain or Rome, but this would have meant working in another language and I was still prudent enough to realise that suddenly to plunge into the full-scale study of theology at forty-eight years of age was going to stretch whatever ability I had to the full without a language problem. I spent a lot of time making enquiries and writing to universities in the British Isles and on the Continent. No one in England seemed to know much about it or how to proceed to obtain a Catholic theology degree. Then, I do not remember how, it was brought to my attention that Heythrop, the Jesuit College at Enstone near Oxford, was just starting to take women students.

Heythrop was then a Pontifical Athenaeum, which meant it was entitled to give Roman degrees, including the Licentiate in Sacred Theology (S.T.L.). In due course I went for an interview. The college, situated right in the country, up a five-mile drive, was a converted stately home. I felt very small as I stood on the huge doorstep, but not in the slightest deterred. The Dean of Studies, who interviewed me, was a typical Jesuit: academic, cultured, he was polite and warmly welcoming. But he seemed to do everything he could, not so much to put me off, as to frighten me off. By the time he had finished on 'thought structures' etc., the impression I had was that they would be talking a language of which I would not know a word, that I really was inadequately qualified. Nevertheless, nothing that he said had the slightest effect on me; it caused not a ripple of misgiving. I had learned to know the Spirit, to listen to him. As the Dean talked, I sounded the depth of the Spirit, I looked within, but there was not so much as a stirring of that peace, a waver of deviation. The Holy Spirit holds you to the course that God has set with a tranquillity that is absolute. You do not look at yourself, if you did you would immediately be overcome with misgivings, you turn to the Spirit who makes God's will known to you by the unstirring deepness of his peace. There was no fear, no misgiving, no doubts, at my own inadequacy which, on the natural plane, was only too apparent. Not a breath of wind, not a ripple stirred the surface. I knew God was holding me to my path, that I was walking towards him. Even the Dean's grudging admission: 'I won't say no', left me unmoved. I am sure he accepted me against his better judgment, under compulsion from the Holy Spirit who was carrying me on the wings of his will.

Going to Heythrop to study theology was stepping out into a complete unknown. I knew nothing of the work requirements or the environment I would be entering which, at that time, was more in the nature of a seminary. Moreover, it meant burning my boats. I had to leave my job, my sole source of income other than dividends of a couple of hundred pounds or so inherited from my mother. I had to sell the house in order to pay the very modest college fees. I might emerge four years later with a degree, but my home would have gone and there would be no possibility of getting another. None of this worried me or perturbed me. It was not hard to do. Indeed the way was filled with light and every step was eased. Having been refused a grant by the Local Education Authority in London, I was fortunate enough to obtain a very small one from a charitable organisation promoting initiatives by women. This I probably obtained through being the first laywoman to enter the field of Catholic theology in England, although many had done so on the Continent.

As I look back now, I wonder at the ease with which I ousted N. from his home. Having suggested the step, he had continued to encourage me, assuring me that he would be able to find himself accommodation when the time came. Tardiness had always been characteristic of N. and, sure enough, when the time came and I was packed up ready, N. still had not found anywhere to go, although he again assured me that, if the worst came to the worst, he could always share a flat with some of his numerous rugger-playing friends. In the end the furniture van came and I climbed into the cab with them for the seventy-mile drive, leaving the house empty except for N., his bed, a chair and the kitchen cooker. He loved his home, he did not want to go, and there he dallied until the bitter end. Eventually, after a few days of what must have been very sad solitude, he went off to his friends, where he knocked about for two or three years, before settling successfully in the city and then happily marrying.

At the time I had no compunction about depriving him of his home. I was acting under the impetus of an irresistible drive which I knew to be a manifestation of God's will for me; I can well understand how Cornelia Connelly is said to have stepped over her son when he threw himself down to try to prevent her from going off to a convent. N. had to be sacrificed to God's will; between his eighteenth and twenty-third year he lost everything. First he lost his father, then his brother got married and, although he had not seen much of him since he went to Dartmouth, from then on he saw even less, then his mother, inexplicably distrait, became absorbed in a multitude of new interests, including the institute which demanded a lot of time and attention. Finally, he was deprived of his home to which he was deeply attached. My heart aches for him now in a way it never did at the time; of course if it had, I would not have been able to act as I did. If God hardened my heart, then he protected N., who had to suffer the consequences, bringing him safely through the vicissitudes of some uneasy years, apparently unscathed and all the better for his enforced independence. We always kept in close contact. He used to come and stay at Heythrop and we would meet in London. One parting at a tube station is imprinted on my memory when, as he stepped onto the descending escalator, he turned to wave good-bye; his sadness was written on his face. Never did he utter a word of complaint or reproach. I think he took the attitude that I had worked hard to provide for them in the past and that it was only fair that now I should be allowed to do what I so obviously wanted and felt drawn towards.

Chapter 6

When the pantechnicon containing four men, myself and all my worldly possessions, swung into the approach to Heythrop and drew up like a pebble on a vast expanse of beach, I felt even smaller than when I had come for my interview. In my mind I assessed the situation: what was I doing there and what was going to happen? I had no conception of what the work was going to entail or whether I would be intellectually capable of assimilating it. I was returning to study after a break of over thirty years, I knew very little of university life, nothing of seminary life. I was going to be considerably older than the other students; I would be one of four women, the other three being religious, in an all-male stronghold; I would be the first and only laywoman, possibly the only lay student. No power on earth could have got me into that hive of Jesuits, no power on earth did get me there – only a divine power, peacefully assuring, instilling a gentle, imperturbable confidence; there were no misgivings, only an eagerness to step into that unknown wherein was stored food for my hungry intellect.

Our home, which had been a gardener's cottage, adjoined some derelict outhouses and looked out onto the walled kitchen garden, now a luxuriant mass of weeds and brambles with shoulder-high willow herb and rhubarb. It was hidden amongst the trees and pathways, five minutes from the college, and in the afternoons when, in those leisurely surroundings, no one did any work, professors could be seen strolling in pairs or singly, taking their constitutional. The conditions were ideal for study, a little hermitage, surrounded by the stillness and peace of acres and acres of wild parkland, yet within a few paces of the college with all its activity. Early in the morning we would wend our way across to the chapel for Mass, returning an hour or so later for breakfast; in summer I often had breakfast outside, sitting on the stone wall looking into the walled garden, still lovely in all its wild disorder. I spent many hours of study outside in that idyllic environment. Our solitude, however, was more often than not invaded. Students and professors frequently dropped in or came for a meal and we had many visitors, family and friends, some of whom would stay for a few days. There were times when we were so overwhelmed with domestic commitments that it interfered with study. In general, though, it was a paradisiacal interlude, cut off and sheltered from the normal run of life with all its distractions and demands, free to absorb and nurture the seed of revelation as it pushed its way through the muddy soil of the intellect. It soon became apparent one had to exercise a certain amount of discernment: nevertheless, here was the authentic doctrine – even if one had sometimes to abstract from a professor's accretions – here, at last, was *what the Church teaches*.

When the removal men had gone, I was left surrounded by packing cases, in the company of innumerable spiders of all shapes and sizes, a toad that sat on the backdoor step and owls hooting in the trees. However, my blissful solitude lasted only two days before N. and the sister who was to live with me arrived, followed by an influx of professors and others coming for meals or to be put up for a few days. At the same time, that professor with an alien tongue, the Dean, gave me a volume of philosophy and told me to write an essay on the Four Causes. I had no idea what they were. It took me eleven days of extremely hard and concentrated work to read the book, make notes and write an eleven-page essay which, as the Dean drily pointed out, merely summarised the book. However, it was a beginning and I had found it fascinatingly interesting, although the sheer mental effort required to assimilate that first taste of philosophy somewhat alarmed me. Even here, there seemed to be no peace and uninterrupted time to devote to my study. The contacts and distractions I thought I had escaped had followed me. For the sister, coming out of religious enclosure, the new form of life was something to be relished and the opportunities for contacts to be made the most of, added to which she was unaccustomed to housekeeping or cooking which meant a great deal of explanation and instruction was necessary.

For years thought in me had been like a slippery ball, something I had tried so hard to grasp and hold, but which had always eluded me as my hands closed over it. To be able to concentrate without interruption, to hold a subject in my mind until it became almost concrete, to see it fitting into place, was a form of delight to me. I had waited long for it, fought against such odds to try to do it on my own with so little opportunity, so that now that it at last seemed within my reach, I was like a race horse at the starting gate. There was a terrific force and driving power in my mind, an effect of Our Lord's coming. For with the same intensity of love with which my will and heart held him, so did my intellect yearn for him. He was drawing my mind with an insatiable thirst and drive. The result was that when I was employed on a specific assignment, reading and writing for an essay, the drive was so powerful that it eliminated everything else. This was what I had come to Heythrop for and what God was calling me to do. The house became the merest incidental, people and contacts secondary. Hence the constant distraction of not only living with but of constantly having to attend to another person with, at that time, numerous needs, together with an influx of visitors, the brunt of which again fell on my shoulders as being the one who was competent in housekeeping, had a profound effect on me. Added to all that I realised that not only was I going to be studying theology but, at the same time, I was going to have to teach myself a considerable amount of philosophy. As an experiment, apart from which I would not have been there, students without a previous philosophy degree were being accepted for the theology course, but this only applied to a minority. Nearly all would have done their philosophy and many of the Jesuit students had second degrees as well. In this, apart from any other considerations, I was going to be at a great disadvantage. I was being thrown in at the deep end; without any preparation suddenly plunged into a highly intellectual environment, expected to be able to hold my own with minds already conditioned by many years of study. For the first time since Our Lord's coming, I knew fear. I had several attacks which started as a queer draining, sinking sensation in the stomach, as if my pulse was getting weaker and was going to stop – and with it came fear. It may primarily have been a primitive fear of death – but the fear that took form was always that I was going to be frustrated in the thing I had to do. I was being driven by a terrific force, but there was an obstacle that impeded that impetus – and the obstacle was all the distractions and extra housework with which I was being saddled. The fear was that my body would not be able to sustain the impetus of my mind, because external circumstances would put too much burden on it. It was the same as it had been all along: the demands of people seemed to be interfering with the demands of God.

Although my basic purpose and underlying confidence never faltered, at first I was very frightened of my own inadequacy. It took me several weeks to adapt to the sudden transition to violent intellectual activity; I felt my brain would crack under the strain of trying to get it round new concepts and terminology in a sufficiently orderly fashion to be able to write essays. However, once term started, the distractions and visitors diminished and, when the lectures were in full swing, I took to it like a duck to water and never flagged. That is not to say I did not have to work hard. All the time I was studying, God continued to attract and draw my intellect, which gave me terrific motivation and power of concentration, but he did not do the work for me. Always, whatever the specific course, the subject matter gripped my mind, which meant I never tired or got bored. Consequently, I was able to work extraordinarily long hours with unabated concentration. My interest never lessened, it was held spellbound all the time. This was what enabled me to complete the course successfully, and it was the work of the Holy Spirit. During the five years that I was at Heythrop I had to work exceedingly hard. I laboured ceaselessly all the time. I often had to strive for understanding, sometimes wresting it from God on my knees, yet the more I laboured, the more I was given, and the more I acquired, the more I thirsted for yet more.

At the end of the first year we were examined on most of the fourteen basic courses which we had completed. One of the professors, full of good intentions, had made a careless but irrevocable mistake. Chatting to me at the coffee break one day, he had said apologetically that the courses were designed for much younger minds. Until then I had thought success or failure would depend entirely upon innate intelligence, of which I hoped and trusted that, with the goading of the Holy Spirit, I had sufficient. Now it dawned upon me that my intellectual ability could be impaired with age: I might not be able to remember sufficiently for examination purposes. As I tried to revise the courses, in itself an almost impossible task, I became increasingly panic stricken and, when it came to the actual exams, I invariably wasted a considerable amount of precious time breaking through my initial paralysis. On one occasion it was forty minutes before I could write a word, although it was a paper I could deal with quite easily. Nevertheless, the results were satisfactory and I even came out top in one of the papers. However, I never managed to uproot the seed which had been sown and, by the time it came to the finals, it had grown into a flourishing plant.

Although I was no longer self-conscious, I still suffered from an inherent inadequacy as regards the spoken word; I was, and still am, tongue-tied. I knew what gift I had was literary and I found I could write at length, in fact at too great length, on almost any subject. I therefore disliked seminars and sat through most without contributing a word; my marks in this respect must have been abysmal, but I made up for it in my written contributions and essays for which I got consistently good ratings. Although my verbal input was practically nil, at least twice I was told I had obtained top marks for the written work of the seminar. I did not find the groping discussion of the other students in seminars helpful, preferring the clear exposition of the professor's lecture. Most significantly, I still suffered from an inhibition regarding public speaking, which had started at school when a teacher had mockingly drawn attention to the inadequacy of my diction, never very good, but further impaired by having to wear braces on top and bottom teeth. No doubt due to the psychological stress to which I had been subjected it came to a head towards the end of my secretarial career. I was sufficiently competent at my work to be able to take verbatim minutes and read them back fluently. One day the man for whom I worked asked me to take down a letter dictated over the telephone by a confrère. I took the letter down in shorthand without any problem, but when the voice at the other end of the line asked me to read it back, I was paralysed with nerves and could not speak. I could have read it all back without hesitation but, because I was trembling and my heart was beating furiously, I could not get any words out; I had to pretend I could not read it, letting not only myself but my boss down lamentably. I made up my mind that never again would I allow myself to get into such a humiliating position. I would never undertake any work which might entail having to speak or read anything out in public. That meant I would not do any minuting work, because the secretary is frequently called upon to read back what has been said or even to read the minutes from the previous meeting. This would be my guiding principle, regardless of promotion or other inducements.

When I entered the institute I was firmly set in this mould and nothing less than my love for God could have induced me to subject myself to the misery and humiliation of my weakness. I had to call upon all my faith in and love of God to get me through the long prayer of admission into the training period, then called the novitiate, which had to be recited in chapel before fifty or so members. Although I managed to get through it, there was no alleviation of my misery. I then found myself having to take my turn as cantor in the recitation of the Office at group meetings. As it was then chanted and as I had no ear, my affliction was even more acute.

Whilst at Heythrop it reached crisis point. The sister with whom I shared the cottage was very involved in ecumenical work and I had gone with her to a unity week service in one of the local churches. I was sitting with the speakers and, when they learned that I was a member of a secular institute, they suggested that at the end I should say a few words on the subject. The combined effect of being asked to speak and having it thrust upon me with no time to prepare rapidly reduced me to a state in which I was shaking so much that my teeth were chattering. The organisers, not being able to ignore my plight, kindly pointed out that, if I did not wish to speak, it was not necessary. However, I realised that it was now or never. Unless I went through with it this time, I was finished. In future I would be even more afraid and would never be able to make the break-through. So I got up and went to the rostrum. I have no idea what I said, but I spoke for a few minutes. That was the turning of the tide, but I still had to go through a painful struggle to overcome my nerves and general aversion to making my voice heard in any gathering of people.

Writing was my medium; I had always known it was the gift I had been allotted and I wanted to use it. However, towards the end of my time at Heythrop, it was pointed out to me that, before one can write, one needs to have taught, because it is in assembling the material that one's own ideas are clarified. For me, without a teaching degree, this could only mean lecturing. So, one of the first things I did after leaving Heythrop was to enrol in adult education classes in public speaking. These certainly helped and gave me enough confidence to promote my own courses of lectures. Enamoured of my subject matter, I found that it took over and carried me through and before long I was able to deliver an hour's lecture with only minor initial qualms if it was a particularly large or unfamiliar audience.

It was a long, hard struggle in which God's help was concealed. I was not aware of it, as I was in other areas, and yet without his help I could never have confronted and overcome the panic which would overwhelm me. One will do anything for love, and the taking upon myself of something so repugnant and traumatic was the measure of my love for God. Because in the first place it was demanded of the institute situation in which he had placed me, I could only assume it was part of his will for me. It was therefore a

142

matter of obedience to God and the institute way of life. For love, there was no option – and that, of course, was the grace. My love of God itself was pure gift, as was what it drove me to do. I did not, however, manage to conquer my misgivings in respect of my memory. Here I had a two-fold disadvantage: the obliteration of the past at Our Lord's coming with a subsequent inability to look behind and the Heythrop trauma. The result is that I never speak without writing everything down in full. I may, to a large extent, have overcome my fear of opening my mouth in public, but I still need my props: a full and complete text of what I am going to say. Without that I would be afraid of drying up, my mind going blank. It is an abyss into which I have not yet dared to step, nor does it seem to me that God has called me to do so. I know that I have no verbal eloquence or even ability and therefore invoke that very accommodating virtue, prudence. God's ways indeed are strange and wonderful: I ended up actually earning my living in the very way which I had promised myself I would never undertake, even as a subsidiary element of my work.

On a natural level, that is abstracting from the immediate years after Our Lord's coming when I hardly inhabited this world, the Enstone Heythrop was, I suppose, the happiest two years of my life. Being a combination of university and seminary in the most beautiful natural setting, it fulfilled all my needs. The Jesuits are very efficient and thorough educators; their professors were erudite men who had undergone a prolonged period of training, including several years at universities. Within the first two years we were acquainted with the basic elements of the main areas of theology and scripture studies. The college still functioned under strict discipline. Jesuit scholars had to wear their gowns for Mass, which all had to attend early in the morning, also for the weekly Benediction, at which it was very moving to hear the strong swell of their voices in 'Be Thou my vision'. Every

143

Jesuit's room contained a prie-dieu and each Jesuit had a spiritual director to whom he made a regular manifestation. Professors wore their gowns for lectures and were to be seen pacing outside the lecture hall door prior to the lecture; they were never late. Women were still debarred from the refectory, which meant that we had to have our lunch with the secretaries in one of the reception rooms. When, with much ado, we were finally admitted to the refectory, it was only to discover that it was the thin edge of the wedge which was going to transport us to London and transform us into a secular university. I was witnessing the last throes of a truly Catholic educational institution, administered by a religious community as a religious institution, the majority of students being Jesuits, the rest religions of other Orders. Money was very secondary, fees being small and waived or vastly reduced when confronted by need. The atmosphere was relaxed and friendly – or so it seemed to one on the periphery of the actual community.

A strange lacuna was that during the first year there were no tutorials and the very few there were during the second year related only to the topic in hand. Not until we moved to London was each student allotted a tutor responsible for their general welfare. This meant that, during the first two years, for the non-Jesuits there was no counselling of any kind and no overall support as regard one's work or problems in that or any other direction. The result was a certain amount of mental and spiritual indigestion. It was impossible to assimilate and digest the vast amount of material with which we were fed, and there was no doctor to give a diagnosis and provide a soothing panacea. Separated from the rest of the students by my age, marriage, female sex and lay status, and still stunned from the shock of God's coming five years previously, it was hardly surprising that I made no close friends. Mixing easily enough with everyone at a superficial level, I was completely happy and absorbed in the work and the contacts it generated. In the academic milieu I was like a fish in water, yet at the same time I was desperately lonely. I longed, not for a professor, but for a priest with whom to discuss the deeper implications of what I had absorbed. It was ironical that, surrounded as never before by priests, there was no *priest* to talk to, no offer of pastoral assistance. I used to go regularly to the Jesuit allocated to hear the parish confessions, but during those two years I received not one word other than those of absolution. My own director, except for brief visits to England, was in Rome. Although in general he was of immense help, there was neither time nor opportunity to enter into the lengthy correspondence which would have been necessary were he to be of any help in this particular area. For instance, *why* was the insidiously attractive theology of Tillich not acceptable? No one was going to tell me, unless I was way offstream. We were not being told the answers, we were being taught to do theology, to think it not for ourselves – but without a kindred mind against which to rub, it was a lonely task. Added to which I sometimes caught nuances, whiffs of thinking which my inner spirit refused to accept. Like undigested material it would rise to the surface to be spat out. This created a certain amount of tension, because I found it hard to believe that my intuition might possibly be more sound than a professor's reasoning and academic experience. The Holy Spirit gives to the faithful in varying degrees the ability to intuit doctrinal error, but to conceptualise it is quite another matter.

Throughout, conceptualisation has been my problem. The whole content of doctrine, what the Church teaches, was there, given in the moments of Our Lord's coming, yet inexpressible. The content had been given, but the conceptualisation was left to me. It is a slow, laborious process – a working backwards from a more perfect, non-conceptualised knowledge to a deficient rationale. It is not a matter of reasoning in order to arrive at knowledge and insight, but of struggling to express what is already known and 'seen'. Mysticism is often set in opposition to doctrine. It is not so; they are a unity, two sides of the single coin of the faith which the Church teaches. Genuine mysticism – that which originates from God – is doctrine experienced and lived; doctrine is mysticism explained. What had been given in my experience of God was easily recognisable as in exact conformity with scripture and the Church's Eucharistic doctrine. I had *experienced Truth* and, in so doing, *knew God*. That experience provided a rule of faith, a scale on which to weigh doctrine. I knew whether or not it balanced, but to know *why* was a different matter and often a hard struggle. Much of my theology was done on my knees; thrown back upon God, I had to wrest from him the answer to each problem as it arose.

Although in going to Heythrop I had escaped from the office, which had always been a source of income rather than a chosen career, secretarial duties still pursued me. During the time that I was at Heythrop I became secretary to the Institute Regional Council and also the International Council, which meant attending council meetings, sometimes abroad, to take the minutes, together with many hours afterwards transcribing and typing them. In the long vacation at the end of my first year, I went from the intellectual gymnastics of the fourteen courses and subsequent exams, to the Institute Chapter for renewal of the Constitutions, where I was in charge of secretarial arrangements. As the help I was given was very inadequate it meant bearing the brunt of reporting the proceedings and producing the typescripts of the finalised texts. The Chapter lasted a week and I remained a further two weeks completing my work. The result was I had very little rest in the vacation and returned for my second year beginning to show physical symptoms of stress.

146

At the end of the second year, Heythrop became part of London University and the Enstone college closed. After term was ended in June 1970, and my companion had returned to her London convent, I stayed on in the cottage, reluctant to leave what had been the milieu of so much happiness. The college was deserted except for a few Jesuits busy with the final cleaning and packing up. Already the atmosphere had changed; strangers were prowling in the grounds and some of my cases, which had been stored in the outhouses adjoining the cottage, were broken into and rifled. Clinging lovingly to the cottage, which was now more in the nature of a hermitage, I outstayed my welcome. I had become a nuisance and embarrassment; they wanted me out so that they could complete the clearing up of the estate. Eventually I sadly departed for London, sending the furniture into store.

Chapter 7

With the decision to move to London, I was confronted with two serious problems: where to live on my meagre resources and how to pay the vastly increased college fees. Again, the path was made smooth for me. Surprisingly, since I was now fifty, Oxford County gave me a grant, provided that the college would have the fees, which they generously agreed to do, with the effect of a bursary. The Oxfordshire Awards Panel before which I had to go consisted of two men and a woman, and it was the latter who opposed my application, reckoning how many years I would have before retiring, but the men must have out-voted her. The grant was given on the understanding that I would be taking the London B.D., normally a three-year course. However, I was now two years through my four-year Roman S.T.L. A compromise was arrived at between the college and university authorities, by which those of us in the middle of our S.T.L., ten Jesuits, two sisters and myself, would be allowed to complete it concurrently with the three-year B.D. course. That meant three years in London, a total of five years with the two years at the old Heythrop. The completion of our S.T.L. was a concession on the part of the university authorities because, as part of London University, Heythrop was no longer allowed to give the Roman S.T.L. There was no Catholic faculty of theology in the university, although they (Heythrop) retained their own Catholic professors and were therefore able to supply a Catholic background and interpretation. The college made the condition that those of us who obtained both degrees under these exceptional circumstances were not to be allowed to use them concurrently on any official or printed matter. We could use either, but not both together.

I took the B.D., not because I wanted to, but because it was the only way in which to complete my S.T.L., which was the only degree which would satisfy me – it was also considerably more comprehensive. On principle I did not go to the B.D. graduation ceremony. Remnants of the ancient monastic origins still remained, at least at Oxford, where I had seen N. kneel to receive his history degree. There would, of course, have been no problem with a secular degree, but theology bears faith implications. I was quite happy to be qualified in non-Catholic theology, but I drew the line at bending the knee before a representative of any other than the true Church.

The problem of accommodation was solved by the wonderful generosity of the Servite Sisters in North London who made room for me in their convent, refusing to take any payment during the two years I was with them. It was an ideal situation for me, in which I had the best of both worlds. Sharing their living conditions, yet extraneous to the actual community and therefore without any of its responsibilities, I revelled in the ordered background to my studies and being able to join in the daily Mass, Office and other occasions of prayer. The chapel on the premises, with the opportunity for prayer before the Blessed Sacrament at any time, was a luxury I had never previously experienced and of which I took full advantage, especially late at night. I spent two extremely happy years there. The sisters overwhelmed me with kindness and subjected me to a spoiling which I did not deserve and have never been able to repay. Having seen how the aftermath of Vatican II changed the lifestyle of the Jesuits, I now saw the same thing happening with the sisters.

Whilst I was there, there was a transformation to a much more open and less restricted form of life. Inevitably there was some imbalance, and my impression from the sidelines was that of an overstress on community and, to my sorrow, partly due to the elimination of periods of silence, the loss of any aura of recollection within the convent.

However, in spite of their kindness, all was not smooth nor easy as far as I was concerned; there were difficulties in other areas. I was heavily committed in the institute with secretarial and other duties, which were very time consuming, and at the beginning of 1971 my brother was taken into intensive care with heart trouble, necessitating visits to him and nights spent with my sister-in-law. He seemed to make a good recovery but, the day before the fortnight's revision for important S.T.L. exams was to begin, he died very suddenly. Again, I had to stay with my sister-in-law, going up north with her for the funeral. This seriously disrupted my study and the exams, creating acute tension which subsequently manifested itself in a very sore skin complaint in my mouth, for which I had to attend a skin specialist regularly for the next ten years. He put me onto cortisone and barbiturates, against the soporific effects of which I had to fight for the rest of my time at Heythrop. At the time he insisted I have a term's absence from college. Only when I stopped, and was able to sleep continually for three or four days, did I realise how exhausted I was. I was away thirteen weeks, five of which I spent in a cottage in Devon. The final obstacle came in 1973, during my last term at Heythrop. I slipped a disc in my back, the result of which was excruciating pain down one leg which never left me day or night. I could not bend or put on my shoes or stockings and could only lie, more than sit, on a chair. There was no respite. Drugs were ineffective and I could not sleep at night, often going down to the chapel in the early hours. As it was so near my finals, things moved quickly, and after a few weeks the disc was removed. The pain, however, continued for several weeks after the operation.

All the time, of course, I had to continue with my revision. I finally arrived back at college three weeks before the finals. Needless to say, the weeks of pain and the debilitating effects of the operation all added to the growing sense of panic at the approaching finals. These were nine three-hour papers, some grouped so that there was no time in between to refresh and switch one's mind. Nor did the three hours give time to do justice to the papers, which often had to be handed in unfinished. As the exam days passed, we seemed to be moving from paper to paper faster and faster and my panic grew accordingly, until it overwhelmed me. The subject matter was far too extensive, even in perfect conditions, to revise and to treat adequately in the time allotted. Almost paralysed with the accumulation of stress and fear of my own inadequacy, it required all the courage I had to continue to enter the examination room. All I knew was that I must write from the moment the paper was opened, and keep writing until the time was up, not a minute to spare to plan, marshal one's thoughts, let alone plumb the depths. Mercifully I never had to look at the drivel I am sure I wrote. A few could not stand the pace and fell by the wayside. Since then the system has been changed, so that it is now much less stressful.

Once my days of study were over, I had to decide how I was going to put to use my new qualifications. How a female theologian was to be employed was obviously something of a puzzle to the college. Since I had no teaching qualification, the easy solution of Head of R.F. was ruled out. One Jesuit parish priest suggested I become his housekeeper and, as inducement, assured me I would be able to do some catechising; the Dean of Studies suggested I take the vacant position of secretary to Professor Dunstan of King's College, who assured me *some* theology would be involved. I was later in touch with the Benedictines of Ampleforth regarding C.O.R.A.T., the renewal scheme they were establishing for contemplative nuns. This was to be in the nature of both theological input and administrative help. I was very interested and would dearly have liked to have been involved in drawing up and presenting to the nuns some theological material, but the Benedictines were only prepared, and indeed were eager, to offer me an administrative post which would have meant bringing the nuns up to date on such matters as finance, pensions, welfare, etc., together with general secretarial duties, duplicating the theological material compiled by the Benedictines, etc. All these I turned down. I had not set out on an entirely new path and laboured lovingly at theology for five years only to return to where I had been before. I realised that if I wanted to do theology I was going to have to fight for myself and make my own way. There was, however, a set-back which I had to accept. It was suggested by the institute that I work for a year in a secretarial capacity at the head office of Servite Houses. This was intended to fulfil the two-fold purpose of giving me a break from mental activity and helping the Housing Association in the office reorganisation which was going on at the time. By the end of the year I was chafing at the bit. It was time to be about the business that I had to do. I knew I was not where God wanted me.

It was now 1974, a time when many, especially young people, were abandoning their faith to pursue Eastern gurus, when Eastern prayer techniques were infiltrating Christian institutions and prayer groups and when some theologians, trying to integrate Eastern and Christian doctrine, were propagating a great deal of confusion. It struck me as tragic that anyone should turn away from the Church, the guardian of a mysticism so real that it is concretised in the Incarnation, in order to search, for the most part, Hinduism whose doctrine is professedly founded on myth and

Buddhism which does not profess to know anything of a deity or to be more than a way of life. Christianity is a mystical religion, certainly veiled in faith, but a veil that has been partially lifted by the great body of Christian mystics throughout the ages. Only Christianity holds the key to the mystical problem: the immanence of the transcendent God; in other words, how a transcendent God who is totally Other can be experienced explicitly by the mystic, implicitly by the graced individual, without their losing their identity and being subsumed into God. Only Christianity has the answer. And the answer is, of course, Christ. He is the bridge, the only bridge, who unites God and man in mystical union. The mystical traditions of the great non-Christian religions can be seen to be striving towards the answer to which they are so close, yet can never attain without the enlightenment of revelation. Without it, they must inevitably take refuge in pantheism. The Incarnation is the key to any genuine mysticism – it is that which both makes it possible and explains it.

God has always sent us mystics, people who observe in themselves and map out for us the movements and development of the inner life of grace, and he continues to do so. For historical reasons, for a long time the Church has failed to avail herself of the mystical treasury which she enshrines and the inspiration and understanding of which is there for the taking. Now, God in his mercy, has recalled us to an appreciation of and thirst for mysticism. That interest needs directing to the unsurpassable truth and richness of the Christian tradition. That, in a very small way, is what I set out to do.

It meant I had to draw up my own programme of courses and promote them. My first attempt was whilst I was still working for Servite Houses. By putting up notices in churches and libraries I managed to collect a group of about eight interested people and, in a room kindly lent by C.H.A.S., gave them a course of talks on Christian mysticism running over several weeks. After completing my time at Servite Houses, I continued on the same lines of self-promotion, getting together small groups in different locations and earning a very small income. At the same time I scanned the advertisements and wrote innumerable letters applying for lecturing and other positions, without success. I then tried all the local London Education Authorities, suggesting they include in their Adult Education programme one of the four options of which I had drawn up an outline: Christian Doctrine, Ecumenical Studies, Biblical Studies, Christian Mysticism. I was delighted when Ealing Education Authority selected Christian Mysticism. It could, of course, no longer be treated in isolation, but had to be related to the Eastern traditions and techniques which were proving so attractive. So I had to acquire and transmit a basic knowledge of Hindu, Buddhist and Sufi mysticism. As I was totally ignorant of these, it necessitated a great deal of hard work and reading. The course was therefore very extensive. Starting with definitions of mysticism, then dealing with non-Christian mysticism before beginning the Christian, it took two years to complete. It went through twice with small groups of faithful followers. Then, when the financial cuts started to take their toll, something so obscure as mysticism was one of the first casualties.

However, it had given me confidence and forced me to acquire a lot of knowledge and experience which would not otherwise have come my way. It had been a breakthrough in getting such a course accepted and put on single-handed, rather than being sponsored by the diocese or some other body. I was anxious to remain independent. I had seen the red light as regards academic and catechetical circles and I wanted to be free to express myself in what I considered to be orthodox categories without being pressurised into stances which I would have found unacceptable. From then on I took whatever came as being the way in which God was calling me to use my qualifications – one-off lectures, training courses for the Servite sisters and the institute, weekends on Christian Mysticism at Ealing Abbey Prayer Centre, etc. Apart from the training talks, this has concentrated on mysticism and the Christian mystics.

Whilst my interest was essentially dogmatic, the intellectual expression of Truth, God's self-revelation, as channelled through scripture and the tradition of the Church, it is hardly surprising that I found myself specifically drawn towards mystical theology, the charting of the soul's awareness of the grace activity taking place within it, the history of the love affair between the soul and its Maker. It provided an outlet for those things I could not divulge. I could not speak about my personal experience of God, but I could speak through the great mystics. I could use them to say the things I wanted to say and, of course, to say it far better, more comprehensively and with deeper insight than I could ever hope to do.

It required initiative and perseverance to establish myself and create a little perch from which to sing my praises of the God who had revealed himself to me as the God of scripture and tradition, as the One whom the Church proclaims. I had to work extremely hard to draw up such extensive courses from scratch and then, often, to condense material drastically where shorter courses or a one-off talk on some mystic or complex aspect of mysticism was required. I had to overcome my natural shyness and inhibitions, knocking on presbytery and vicarage doors in order to hand in my self-promotion material. I earned only sufficient so that, with what was beginning to come in from what I had inherited, I was just able to keep my head above water. Although the whole enterprise was something entirely out of character, I had no qualms and was able to carry it through easily and peacefully. I had no faith in myself, but I had boundless faith in my subject matter, and it was that which supported me as on wings.

Epilogue

In this two-fold account of my life, each part only makes sense in the context of the whole; neither part should be viewed without reference to the other. 'Before' is the natural, upon which the grace of 'After' builds. Grace abounds, and God is the architect, but he works through *us*, settling the account through human channels, allowing us to make and receive reparation for our sins and failings and those of others, reparation which is weighed down and running over with the abundance of grace. Just as St. Peter was given the opportunity to make reparation for his threefold denial of Christ in his threefold affirmation of love, so are similar opportunities offered to us. And just as, with the coming of the Holy Spirit, the sand that was Peter was transformed into rock, so it is with us. In an extraordinary and fitting way After is a time of reparation for the evils and reward for the good of Before. The grace of After takes its shape from Before.

Those who in any way injured me in Before unknowingly repay the debt in After, in a measure full and running over, and I, likewise, am given opportunities for making amends. For the Jesuit whose social engagement caused him to forget me in my dire pastoral need, the Order imparted the precious gift of its sound theological learning, housed me for two years, and for three years bore the brunt of half my college fees. For the Carmelite who, in my hour of lonely and desperate need, failed to console me in the name of the Church, the Order, both friars and nuns, rewarded me for work for them with amazing generosity, and it is owing to the generous hospitality of the Carmelite nuns in providing a place of solitude and silence for two months that this account of my life has been written. My relative who, wisely, but perhaps uncharitably, refused to lend what was a trifle in the light of her considerable wealth, weighed the scale down on the other side through her husband, who survived her and by whose will, to my amazement, I inherited sufficient to meet my needs and to substitute for my lack of pension. This is one of the most extraordinary facts of my life. When I abandoned my secretarial career and sold the house in order to go to Heythrop, it was indeed a step in the darkness of faith because, once my days of study were over, I would be left with no home and an income of only a couple of hundred pounds or so from my mother's shares. The prospects for a woman earning her living doing theology were an unknown still to be explored. The outlook for retirement was even more unfavourable, since my only entitlement would be to something between a third and a half of a state pension. My benefactor died in 1972, which meant that by the end of 1973, when I had completed my studies and was thrown back into the world to fend for myself, the money was coming through. With clever investment by N., whose profession it strangely happened to be, it grew so that even when my theological earnings were practically nil, there has always been sufficient for my needs and I have never had to worry. In view of the financial nightmare of my married life, this is to me a constant miracle, pure gift from the bounty of God. True, I risked all to pursue what I saw to be God's will but, as always, God repaid that response to his call in full measure and running over – and through the channel which originally had failed. It is a strange but wonderful fact that, since I took a vow of poverty, I have never had to worry about money, there has always been enough. It is like the widow's cruse – it gets low sometimes but, in a miraculous way, always fills up again.

Another extraordinary turn of events is the way in which the opportunity for academic study, for which thirty years earlier I had yearned but renounced, knowing it would put financial pressure on my father, was given back to me – again in brimming measure. Stimulated and enticed by God, I drew from my theological studies at Heythrop far greater joy and appreciation than any university studies could have given me earlier in my life. They would only have been tributaries of the Source at which I drank deep.

Likewise I, in After, have the opportunity to make reparation and repay the debts of Before. I owe a deep debt of gratitude to the Benedictine who, before receiving me into the Church, stood by, consoling and sustaining me, through the desolation of A.'s death and the three months that followed. I can hardly say that I repaid his ministry to me in full and overflowing measure, but perhaps in some small way in the contact with their Prayer Centre and a certain type of weekend I have helped to initiate. So much had been given me by the Jesuits, that when I left Heythrop I was deeply indebted to them. That has, I think, to a great extent been repaid with literary help given to a Jesuit professor, a privilege and joy initially which, when extended over twelve years, became something of a cross. What more fitting, when the painful skin complaint in my mouth proved so slow to respond to treatment, than to accept the prolonged discomfort as reparation for the frequent harsh and angry words which desecrated Before.

Permanently underpinning all penance and reparation has been the intention of A.'s salvation. Hardly ever conscious, it rests tranquilly and trustfully in the heart of the Saviour, where it was placed that first Sunday.

My greatest sin Before was inordinate love of a person to the exclusion of God. When God's love takes root in us, and we are able to love those we could never have loved before, there are still some we love more than others because we see more of God in them. It is natural for us to be drawn by the good we see, and grace does not destroy nature. So God sent a person to be loved, not inordinately, but entirely according to his law. He sent a holy priest, who was very intellectual and who could give me the help and guidance I needed. I had to learn to love him with a love that was warm, generous, chaste, unpossessive, detached, undemanding, never detracting from but augmenting my love of God; it was not always easy. I had to love him with the same love with which I loved everyone else, charity, God's love which he has poured into me. Reparation for a disordered, illicit love of a person was invited in an ordered, licit love of a person. Thus is love perfected. It is a lesson that is never completed. I am still learning. We can always love more, love better.

All these occasions and opportunities arose without any foresight on my part as to their propitiatory value; they arose spontaneously as I tried to follow God's prompting as I saw it. Only on looking back and seeing the whole does the pattern begin to emerge.

What of now? Well, now is very ordinary. Sometimes, when I consider how the extraordinary has slowly and gradually subsided into the ordinary, I feel a sense of failure, that there must be something wrong somewhere. I seem to have nothing to show for the wonders and graces God worked in my life. In the lives of the saints, initial manifestations of God's grace activity are usually followed by extraordinary gifts, healing, discernment of spirits, supernatural knowledge, obvious answer to prayer and other charisms. In spite of what happened to me, I have no vestige of any extraordinary powers: I am exactly like everyone else

160

– ordinary. In a way this is disappointing. The world is in desperate need. I feel that there should be more spectacular results. Everything is so small and insignificant. I labour hard, but the output reaches the merest handful of people. However, in this I have one great consolation – Our Lady. She was both the most extraordinary and the most ordinary of all the saints. After the extraordinary events of the Annunciation and birth of Our Lord, her life took on a completely ordinary character, no more extraordinary events, no more interventions of God, no miracles to perform, just the role of mother, housewife, and sorrowing companion on the way of the cross: extraordinary ordinariness.

This combination of extraordinariness and ordinariness typical of Our Lady, in whose footsteps I follow, is something which I see as verifying my secular institute vocation. It is surely of the very nature of consecrated secularity: the ordinariness of secularity transformed by the extraordinariness of consecration, the leaven disappearing in the dough, so that without trace it may transform the lump. If, then, in my life the extraordinary has disappeared into the ordinary, it is as it should be, because I know that that ordinariness is still extraordinary. It is extraordinary because of the inner transformation. It is not the visible exterior, but the hidden interior, which is important. Since that first Sunday my inner disposition has never changed. The Holy Spirit is still as much in command as when he first came. By him I am tranquilly governed. That is the real miracle of my life, a constant and enduring miracle.

Written at:
Carmelite Monastery, Dolgellau, Wales
1.2.86 to 2.3.86

Afterword by Ruth Wilson

Every family has its secrets; it turns out mine had more than its fair share.

When I was seventeen my grandmother, who had been a constant if remote presence in our lives, presented us with her memoir. It contained the shocking revelations that my late grandfather, Alec Wilson, whom I had never met, had been a bigamist with another wife, another family, living somewhere in England. Perhaps it is a testament to my grandmother's impenetrable character that none of us had the courage to ask her any more about it; we just accepted the fact. I often wonder if she secretly wished we had.

Then, five years later, the year after my grandmother died, things got really interesting. Two more distant relatives got in touch with my uncle, Gordon Wilson, stating, 'I think we have the same father', thereby confirming that my grandfather was not a bigamist once, twice or thrice, but four times over, with four wives and four sets of children simultaneously living within a few hundred miles of each other.

As a child my grandfather was never mentioned. He died long before we were born. There were no photographs of him on display; my father never talked of him. When I was about eight years old, while rummaging through my father's desk, I found a tiny black-and-white photo of Alec. I asked my dad who he was. He replied, simply, 'That's my father.' Nothing else was said. That was the last I heard of Alec until my grandmother handed us the memoir about ten years later.

There was an absence at the heart of our family, secrets and mysteries so great and so painful that perhaps it was only right that it was left to the next generation to confront that absence.

At the first extended family gathering, my uncle hosted more than forty Wilsons, each of us wearing name tags labelled 'son of . . .' 'daughter of . . .' Dennis gave a speech; a family tree was drawn; photographs were passed round. We all looked for family resemblances, for common traits. I was relieved to discover that I wasn't the only artist in the family; there were poets, actors and writers. And in fact it turned out my grandfather had himself set up acting troupes with two of his other families. My choice of profession wasn't then a total anomaly. Suddenly I made a bit more sense.

Thanks to the wonderful investigative talents of Tim Crook, an esteemed journalist and lecturer at Goldsmiths College, revelation after revelation about my mysterious grandfather kept coming: his work at MI6, his twenty-three published novels, more details about his family history and personal life. Every time I told anyone outside of the family, the response was one of complete astonishment: how could a man live so many lives in one lifetime? It was a story I never got bored of telling and people didn't seem to tire of hearing. It became clear what happened to my family had resonance beyond those of us directly affected, and so began the long journey of having my grandmother's story dramatised on the BBC.

Neil Blair and Ruth Kenley-Letts took that leap of faith and found the money to start the development process. Anna Symon wrote a remarkable and sensitive adaptation, whereupon our fantastic director Richard Laxton came on board and assembled an extraordinary cast and crew. My family and I couldn't have been in safer hands.

Unsurprisingly, Alec proved the most difficult role to cast. What fascinates me about my grandfather is that everyone who came into contact with him, children, colleagues and wives alike, have incredibly fond memories of him. My grandmother describes him as teaching her 'to love'. I imagine that there was probably something fundamentally broken about my grandfather, but he also had the capacity and the very deep need to love. Iain Glen straddled that line perfectly; there is nothing flippant about his performance, it is as complex and remote as it needs to be.

My family and I will be forever indebted to all those who – with the utmost care, compassion and generosity – worked so hard to bring this story to life.

I realise I have written a lot about my grandfather, which tends to happen when telling my family story. The women – Gladys, Dorothy, Alison and Elizabeth – are often forgotten, ignored for the more mysterious, debonair and dangerous Alec. In trying to dramatise my grandfather, however, we came across a stumbling block: we didn't really know him. Apart from his books we had no record of his voice, no personal account of his life, no justifications for his actions, no real evidence of his work at MI6. He remains a man of mystery. As my grandmother stated: 'He had not only died, he had evaporated into nothing. There was no one left, because where there is no truth there is no person.'

My grandmother, on the other hand, had written this extraordinary memoir, an emotionally raw and brutally honest account of her life. Unlike Alec, I believe my grandmother wanted to be truly known, even if it was only in death. Anna Symon was insistent that Alison's memoir was the best lens through which to tell this story. The drama thus became about those left behind; the damaging effect of secrets and lies within a family and the women who strove to protect their children from the truth. My grandmother describes her memoir as 'a love story'. And this was what became the heart of the drama: despite all the suffering, the betrayal, the poverty, it was a story of family, of faith, of forgiveness and, in my grandmother's words, of 'learning to love'. In dedication to the women, the drama was thus called *Mrs Wilson*.

While Alison became the heart of the drama, Alec became its mystery. Anna had the unenviable task of shaping a three-hour narrative from all the source material. Her challenge was to balance what was true with what was dramatically engaging while being sensitive to the families involved. However, keeping Alison at the heart of the story meant taking dramatic licence. In reality Alison never met Dorothy, but we wanted to dramatise the moment Alison was forced to confront the full brunt of Alec's betrayal. Equally, Alison never forged any documents, but seeing her do so served a number of dramatic purposes: it gave Alison more agency, it made her an active participant in her own denial as well as revealing the contagious effects of secrecy and deception.

Alison stated that if her story was to be told, it should be told in its entirety, 'Before' and 'After'. For me it was vital that we try and serve her whole journey, and that included her dedication to a religious life. However, faith for a largely secular audience is hard to understand, and almost impossible to dramatise, certainly to the sublime levels that my grandmother experienced. Although her faith and forgiveness became the focal point of episode three, we were unable to realise it exactly as she described, a transformation that is of course a deeply private and internal one.

That is why my family and I are so grateful to be able to publish her memoir. Growing up we knew she was a deeply religious woman, but I never understood that she had taken vows, or that she had had what she considered to be intimate and profound experiences with Jesus. It saddens me that she felt she could not share that experience with us when she was alive. Perhaps she feared judgment, perhaps she did not want that relationship tarnished or questioned. It was hers, and hers alone. I remember helping my father clear up her house after she passed away. In the room in which she meditated, for hours a day, there was one window, open, the net curtains blowing lightly in the breeze, the warm June sun filling the room. I was overcome with a profound sense of peace and I wondered if that was similar to the peace she found there.

My grandmother died the year I left drama school. She never saw me act professionally, but I have a feeling that the roles I have been drawn to have been influenced by that memoir. It made me realise that a serious, shy, impenetrable, woman could also be full of passion, of wild imagination, the bearer of extraordinary experience. I only knew Alison Wilson, as the woman we see in episode three, but through this process I had the great privilege of discovering who she was before, when she was nineteen, twenty-nine, thirty-five, forty-five years old. I couldn't remember her voice, and that upset me. I could remember her walk; she always walked with purpose, small steps, head slightly bowed, on a mission. She was always immacutely dressed, hair sprayed into the same bouffant. She was delicate, much more than me, and she had a grace and stillness that I tried to emulate. I often wished I had got someone else to play her. Now, I am so glad I didn't. During filming, there was an extraordinary energy passing through me, something I couldn't control. I had no choice but to give in to whatever happened on the day. It was quite profound. It was an extraordinary privilege being able to sit in my grandmother's experience, to live and breathe as her, something very few people get to do, and I will be forever grateful to all those who made that happen.

By sharing her story, Granny gave us all a gift. It allowed us to break the shame and damage of silence. As fifty family members watched a screening of *Mrs Wilson*, there was a four-minute silence at the end. Family members in tears, hugs between new brothers, new cousins. A shared understanding of what they had all gone through, what their mothers had gone through.

Adapting and performing in *Mrs Wilson* was the most frightening and rewarding experience – more frightening than walking out on to the stage for the first time, or the terrifying experience of seeing my face projected on to a large screen. I felt a responsibility to the people I cared most about: my extended family, my brothers, and to my dad who had survived these events and provided a stable happy home. Perhaps most of all, I felt responsible to my granny, a woman who suffered – like many women of her generation – largely in silence during her lifetime. Yet, she had given me this opportunity to tell her story. I often wonder what she would have thought of the drama. Being terribly English, she would have been mortified by any publicity, but she did want her story to be told. She wanted to give her family an explanation, a means to understand and to forgive. She is the one who brought all of us Wilsons together, weeping and laughing as we explored our family story. She has given us more than she could have imagined. I hope she would have been proud.

Acknowledgements

We want to acknowledge the significant role played by Dennis Wilson, the second son of Alexander's first wife Gladys, after our father's death in 1963. He liaised with Alison, and masterminded the complicated organisation of Alexander's burial service in Portsmouth with characteristic kindness and diplomacy, despite the confusion and grief he must have been feeling at the time. He acted in accordance with Alison's wishes, and helped her protect us, her boys, from the hurtful truth. It is just sad that, after that fleeting meeting over the grave, we remained strangers for most of our lives. We are so glad now to be able to thank him personally for his generosity of spirit in putting our interests, as very young men, above those of him, his mother and his siblings. It seemed to complete the circle when, soon after the reunion of all our father's children in 2007, Dennis undertook the organisation of a headstone for Alexander's grave and the ceremony that we all attended.

We are grateful for the close and trusting friendship that has grown between all our newly found half-siblings – Dennis, Daphne, Mike and Douglas – who have had to come to terms with all the revelations about their family history, and have given us their support and blessing to publish and dramatise Alison's memories of their father.

We are indebted to Professor Tim Crook for his tenacious and indefatigable pursuit of the truth behind our father's many lives – his research has placed our mother's memoir into a context that we could hardly have imagined.

Heartfelt appreciation to Mary Burchfield, dear friend to Alison and fellow Servite, who advised us and gave us her blessing in bringing Alison's story onto screen and into print. The Servites embraced Alison in her neediest hour and gave her love, support and strength to carry out her life's purpose in God.

Thanks to Neil Blair at The Blair Partnership for his continued interest and belief in this project and for being instrumental in the publication of this memoir, as well as the republishing of some of Alexander's novels. Also to Ruth Kenley-Letts of Snowed-In Productions for bringing the drama to fruition, Claire Chesser at Little, Brown Book Group for her care and vision, and Ruth, dear daughter and niece, for giving her heart and soul to her grandmother's story.

Gordon and Nigel Wilson